THEMATIC UNIT
Holocaust

D1504648

Written by Liz Rothlein, Ed. D. and Walter Kelly, M.A.

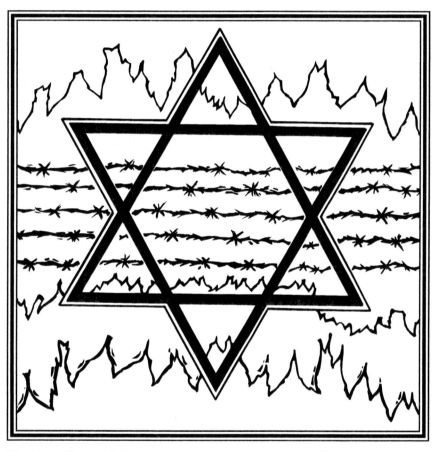

Teacher Created Resources, Inc.
6421 Industry Way
Westminster, CA 92683
www.teachercreated.com
©1997 Teacher Created Resources, Inc.
Reprinted, 2006
Made in U.S.A.
ISBN-1-55734-210-5

Edited by
Walter Kelly, M.A.

Illustrated by
Howard Chaney

Cover Art by
Sue Fullam

Teacher Created Resources

Table of Contents

Introduction

Holocaust is a compelling thematic unit which gives students a realistic view of one of the world's most horrible atrocities—the Holocaust. Its 80 pages are filled with a wide variety of lesson ideas and reproducible pages designed for use with intermediate students at a challenging level. At its core this literature-based thematic unit has three high-quality literature selections—*Daniel's Story, Anne Frank: Beyond the Diary,* and *Elie Wiesel: Voice From the Holocaust.* For each of these books, activities are included which set the stage for reading, encourage the enjoyment of the book, and extend the concepts gained. In addition, the theme is connected to the curriculum with activities in language arts, logic and math, social studies, and art. Many of the activities are additional timesavers for the busy teacher. Highlighting this complete teacher resource are culminating activities. These activities allow students to synthesize and apply the knowledge beyond the classroom.

This thematic unit includes the following:

❑ **Literature selections**—summaries of three books with related lessons (complete with reproducible pages) that cross the curriculum

❑ **Planning guides**—suggestions for sequencing lessons each day of the unit

❑ **Curriculum connections**—poetry and writing suggestions plus activities in language arts, logic and math, social studies, and art

❑ **Group projects**—activities to foster cooperative learning

❑ **Literature-related activities**—additional Holocaust-related books with ideas and activities

❑ **Supplementary activities**—ideas and general activities that relate to the Holocaust

❑ **Culminating activities**—ideas which require students to synthesize their learning

❑ **A bibliography**—a list suggesting additional literature books related to the Holocaust

❑ **Resource materials**—names, addresses, and phone numbers of publishers and companies that have Holocaust materials available

---

To keep this valuable resource intact so that it can be used year after year, you may wish to punch holes in the pages and store them in a three-ring binder.

Introduction (cont.)

Why a Balanced Approach?

The strength of a balanced language approach is that it involves children in using all modes of communication—reading, writing, listening, illustrating, and speaking. Communication skills are interconnected and integrated into lessons which emphasize the whole of language rather than isolating its parts. Balancing this approach is our knowledge that every whole—including individual words—is composed of parts, and directed study of those parts can help a student to master the whole. Experience and research tell us that regular attention to phonics, other word attack skills, spelling, etc., develops reading mastery, thereby completing the unity of the whole language experience. The child reads, writes (spelling appropriately for his/her level), speaks, listens, and thinks in response to a literature experience introduced by the teacher. In these ways language skills grow rapidly, stimulated by involvement and interest in the topic at hand.

Why Thematic Planning?

One useful tool for implementing an integrated and balanced language program is thematic planning. By choosing a theme with corresponding literature selections for a unit of study, a teacher can plan activities throughout the day that lead to cohesive, in-depth study of the topic. Students practice and apply their skills in meaningful contexts. Consequently, they tend to learn and retain more. Both teachers and students are freed from a day that is broken into unrelated segments of isolated drill and practice.

Why Cooperative Learning?

In addition to academic skills and content, students need to learn social skills. No longer can this area of development be taken for granted. Students must learn to work cooperatively in groups in order to function well in modern society. Group activities should be a regular part of school life, and teachers should consciously include social objectives as well as academic objectives in their planning. The teacher should clarify and monitor the qualities of good group interaction just as he or she would clarify and monitor the academic goals of a project.

Four Basic Components of Cooperative Learning

1. *In cooperative learning, all group members need to work together to accomplish the task.*

2. *Cooperative learning groups should be heterogeneous.*

3. *Cooperative learning activities need to be designed so that each student contributes to the group, and individual group members can be assessed on their performance.*

4. *Cooperative learning teams need to know the social as well as the academic objectives of a lesson.*

Historical Background—
The Holocaust

The study of this particular series of events—this era of human history called the Holocaust—is a serious and somber undertaking. Any period of war necessarily involves the deaths of human beings, tragic and inevitably violent. The Holocaust remains a period of brutality so extreme as to constitute nothing less than a debasement of the human spirit. For this reason alone, humanity at large must not forget what happened.

The word *holocaust* means complete destruction of life, usually by fire. Since World War II the term has acquired an even more ominous meaning—the deliberate massacre of six million Jews by the criminal regime of Adolf Hitler and his Nazi Party. As dictator of Germany, one of the most cultured nations of the continent, Hitler's goal was to exterminate all Jews in Europe. He succeeded in killing two-thirds of them before he ended his own life in his bomb-proof bunker under the German Chancellery in Berlin at the end of the war.

Discrimination against Jews began as soon as Hitler took power. Between 1933 and 1939, the Nazis boycotted Jewish businesses, established quotas in the professions and schools, outlawed marriages between Jews and Gentiles, and built Dachau, Buchenwald, and Oranienburg—the first concentration camps. A number of historians date the beginning of the Holocaust itself to the night of November 9, 1938, when Hitler's Storm Troopers went on a rampage, burning 267 synagogues, arresting 20,000 people, and smashing Jewish places of business in an orgy of terror which has since been called *Kristallnacht*—"the night of broken glass." To make the horror of this night even worse, the Nazis then forced the Jews to pay an "atonement" fine of $400 million for the damage which had been done by the regime to the Jews' own property.

For Europe, World War II began in September 1939, with the unprovoked Nazi invasion of Poland. The United States did not enter the war until December 1941. After Germany conquered Poland, Reinhard Heydrich, the Nazi chief of security police, decreed that all Polish Jews were to be confined in a ghetto. Seven hundred thousand Jews died there during the next two years, and when Germany attacked the Soviet Union in June 1941, "strike squads" were sent in against Soviet Jewish citizens. In one atrocity alone, 33,771 Jews were machine-gunned on September 29, 1941.

In January 1942, Hitler called the Wannsee Conference to debate what he called the "final solution of the Jewish question." As a result, during the next three years Jews represented over half of those exterminated in the concentration camps. Gypsies, Slavs, and political prisoners made up most of the rest. Several camps, including Auschwitz, were primarily extermination camps built to kill people. The Nazis were proud of their efficiency in murder, and their methods included using cyanide or carbon monoxide gas, electrocution, and phenol injections, among others.

The concentration camps have come to stand for the worst that humans can do. The Nazis debased and depersonalized the inmates, treating them as though they were not people at all, crowding them into cattle cars, carrying them to the camps without water, food, or sanitary facilities. Camp directors and guards abused them physically and verbally in the worst ways possible, splitting up families, sending men and boys to one place and women and girls to another. In Auschwitz the infamous medical director, Dr. Josef Mengele, deciding with one look at the incoming prisoners which ones would live, personally selected over 400,000 for death and gruesome, horrifying experiments.

Historical Background— The Holocaust *(cont.)*

Everything the Jews owned—money, clothing, books, jewelry, even the hair on their heads and the gold fillings in their teeth—was taken from them. (It is estimated that 72 pounds of gold a day was extracted from prisoners' mouths at Auschwitz alone.) Without blankets or pillows, they slept on wooden shelves, crowded so closely together they could not turn over in their sleep.

Prisoners were forced into slave labor until they could no longer work, and then they were killed. They were identified by the numbers tattooed on their arms. Hundreds of thousands died of typhus or other terrible diseases which flourish when people are forced to live together in unsanitary conditions. Entire families by the thousands were wiped out.

Having no weapons and weakened by disease and malnutrition, the Jews were isolated from other nations, with little resource except to hide if they were able to find sympathetic patrons among the Nazi-dominated populations of Europe. Escape became impossible after the early years. Sixty thousand managed to join with partisan groups who fiercely resisted the Nazis throughout the war, and uprisings occurred in several of the larger ghettos, including the one in Warsaw, Poland.

Those killed included men, women, children, babies, old people, and the handicapped. They included doctors, teachers, librarians, lawyers, business people, store clerks, housewives, students, farmers, and secretaries. People from every walk of life were killed, regardless of who they were, how wealthy or how poor they were, or how good or how bad they were. They were all the same to the twisted criminals who ran the Nazi government and its camps.

The Holocaust is one of the darkest chapters in all of human history—a time when evil was loosed on the inhabitants of a whole continent and became the official government policy of a modern European nation. The enormity of the crimes committed has so traumatized the Western world that shame, sorrow, and guilt still shadow our existence. The written records, photographs of atrocities, and testimonials by those who survived the horrors remain today an overwhelming experience, difficult to face but necessary to confront if new generations are to be spared a return to such debasement of humanity.

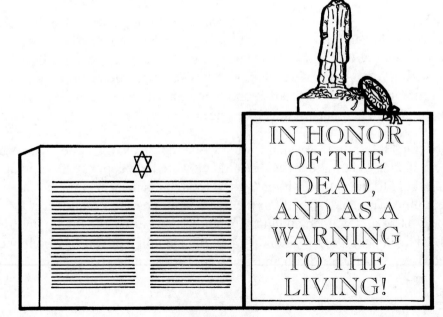

IN HONOR
OF THE
DEAD,
AND AS A
WARNING
TO THE
LIVING!

Daniel's Story

by Carol Matas
(Scholastic, Inc., 1993)

Summary

Daniel, a fictional Jewish boy whose family suffers immensely as the Nazis rise to power in Germany, can hardly remember what his life was like prior to their takeover. He does have a collection of photographs that help him to bring back memories of a happier and safer life; however, as he and his family face the dangers threatening Jews in Hitler's Germany in the late 1930s, his memories begin to diminish. Daniel's family is forced from their home in Frankfurt and sent on a long and dangerous journey—first to Lodz ghetto in Poland and then to Auschwitz, the Nazi death camp. Although many around him lose hope, he is supported by his courageous family and is able to find hope, life, and even love in the midst of despair.

The outline below is a suggested plan for using the various activities that are presented in this unit. You should adapt these to fit your own classroom situation. Prior to beginning the study of the Holocaust, send the letter on page 10 to the parents of your students.

Sample Plan

Lesson I

❏ Read and discuss the dedication page of *Daniel's Story*.
❏ Read Chapter 1 of *Daniel's Story* and assign "Pack Your Bags" (page 13).
❏ Discuss Aunt Leah and Daniel's conversation on page 7 in *Daniel's Story* (see Enjoying the Book, page 8, activity 2).
❏ Continue reading *Daniel's Story* (Part 1—Pictures of Frankfurt). Discuss Daniel's mixed emotions about loyalty to Germany in the face of discrimination against Jews.
❏ Discuss the Evian Conference ("Jews for Sale") and the responsibility of any country to help the oppressed from another country. Can any one country accept all refugees from oppression? Discuss the episode of Daniel wearing the Hitler Youth uniform—Was it wise? dangerous? foolish? Did it help him in any way?

Lesson II

❏ Continue reading *Daniel's Story* (Part 2—Pictures of Lodz).
❏ Assign photo activity (see Extending the Book, page 9, activity 1).
❏ Review history books (see Extending the Book, page 9, activity 3) and assign "What Do the History Books Say?" (page 16).
❏ Discuss the following elements of Part 2:
  -Oma Rachel's disguise—does it remind one of Daniel's wearing of the Hitler Youth uniform?
  -Daniel's mother's foresight in packing warm clothes and boots
  -the symbol of the radio standing for resistance
  -the problems of keeping clean and Daniel's embarrassment when Erika brings Rosa home
  -Rosa's conversation with Daniel about hope (page 56)

-the importance of precious belongings—radio, violin, *The Count of Monte Cristo*, the camera, and the diary
-Review "Glossary" on pages 133–136 of *Daniel's Story* and assign "Holocaust Crossword Puzzle" (page 12).

Lesson III

❏ Continue reading *Daniel's Story* (Part 3—Pictures of Auschwitz).
❏ Review Chronology on page 132 of *Daniel's Story* and assign "Holocaust Time Line" (page 11).
❏ Read the recommended books and react (see Extending the Book, page 9, activity 4).
❏ Discuss feelings and assign "Character Emotions" (page 14).
❏ Discuss the following elements in Part 3:
  -Daniel's determination to stay alive and keep his father alive
  -the Nazis' continual use of music in the camp
  -the brutality of the kapos, actually fellow prisoners
  -the resistance movement within the camp
  -the importance of cameras (as related to history and justice)

Lesson IV

❏ Finish reading *Daniel's Story* (Part 4—Pictures of Buchenwald).
❏ Assign an "Ode to Daniel," (page 15)
❏ Generate a list of what students learned (see Extending the Book, page 9, activity 5.
❏ Discuss the following elements of Part 4:
  -the ruse the prisoners use to retard the construction of the gas chamber at Buchenwald
  -Daniel's desire for blood revenge and his father's reaction
  -Daniel's vow to keep his pictures and not forget
  -Discuss the sequence of events in *Daniel's Story* and assign "Holocaust Events (page 17).

Overview of Activities

Setting the Stage

1. Send a letter such as the sample on page 10 to the students' guardians in which you inform them about what their children will be studying. The study of a topic like the Holocaust is by its very nature a serious undertaking and can be disturbing to impressionable young minds. Family support and prior understanding can be of great value in such a unit. You might also wish to include with the letter a copy of "Historical Background—The Holocaust," pages 5 and 6, to help introduce the tone and content of study.

2. Provide students with copies of pages 5 and 6, "Historical Background—The Holocaust." Read and discuss this together as a class.

3. Read the dedication of *Daniel's Story* and ask the students to interpret what they think it means. Ask them to share what information they have about children throughout history (including those living today) who have not lived in a world of peace and love. In addition to periods of war, they may mention living through natural disasters, child abuse, marital upheavals, etc. Make a list of these perilous times and discuss how such times affect people's lives.

4. Using the information provided in the "Chronology" found on page 132 of *Daniel's Story*, ask the students to create a time line on page 11. Assign small groups of students to each significant historical event and ask them to research that event and complete the questions on page 11. Ask them to be prepared as a group to share their findings.

5. In order to assist the students in better understanding the vocabulary associated with the Jewish culture and the Holocaust, tell them to complete page 12.

Enjoying the Book

1. Read Chapter 1 of *Daniel's Story*. Then discuss the items Daniel has with him in his rucksack. Tell the students to pretend they have to leave their homes and that all they can take with them has to fit into a backpack. Ask the students to make a list of these items on page 13. Will they decide to include food? clothes? books? decorative items? souvenirs? medicine? tools? sewing kit? Some students will have had experience camping and may recall having forgotten to take an important item or two. Ask them to call upon such experience and share it with the class.

2. On page 7 of *Daniel's Story*, when Daniel is having difficulty with Mr. Schneider, his teacher, his Aunt Leah says, "You must show respect for your teachers, Daniel." He replies, "Why? They don't show respect for me." Ask the students to respond to this situation. Who do they think is right and why? How can the situation be resolved?

3. Ask the students to think about different emotions generated and felt throughout the book—hope, disgust, loneliness, anger, fear, hatred, sorrow, love, etc. Ask them to complete page 14.

4. Using the map in *Daniel's Story* as well as other sources, assist the students in locating the main concentration camps that were established by the Nazis.

Overview of Activities *(cont.)*

Extending the Book

1. Daniel feels a need to look at pictures of his life over a period of time so that he can better piece together the events of his life. Ask the students to use real photographs or to illustrate events from the beginning of their lives to present and to put these together in booklets. Have them design covers for the booklets. Then allow students time to share their life events with other students in small groups.

2. Ask the students to write an ode about Daniel. Explain that an ode is a poem that is usually written to honor something or someone and follows guidelines found on page 15—basically an open form with respect to rhyme and stanza but adhering to serious tone and formal language.

3. Obtain history books with varied publication dates from a variety of publishers. Divide the students into small groups. Ask them to review the information in those books which is presented about the Holocaust, using page 16 as a guide. Once reviews are completed, allow time for the students to compare and contrast the information they find.

4. Two of Daniel's favorite books, *The Magic Mountain* by Thomas Mann and *The Count of Monte Cristo* by Alexandre Dumas, are mentioned in *Daniel's Story*. Obtain copies of these books and allow time for the students to read them. Then set aside time for students to share their readings and reactions. Ask them to make comparisons about the events and themes in those books and events and themes in *Daniel's Story*—e.g., injustice, cruelty, revenge, etc.

5. Tell the students to pretend that the current Chancellor of Germany has learned that they have been studying the Holocaust and have just completed reading *Daniel's Story*. He wants to know what they have learned from reading this book. As a group, brainstorm and make a list of things that have been learned. After the list has been generated, ask the students to compose their letters, using a formal letter style.

6. Discuss the many events that take place in *Daniel's Story* and ask the students to complete "Holocaust Events" on page 17. It might help to separate them into events from Frankfurt, events from Lodz, events from Auschwitz, and events from Buchenwald. Such sequencing will aid memory and evaluation for both student and teacher.

7. Request a copy of the video, *Daniel's Story*, that is available from the U.S. Holocaust Memorial Museum, 100 Raoul Wallenberg Place, S.W., Washington, DC 20004 (202) 488-0400. After viewing the video, ask the students to compare and contrast the video and the book.

Parent Letter

_____

_____

_____

Dear Parents:

We are beginning a study of the Holocaust that occurred during the Hitler regime in Germany. As you know, this is a somber period of history to be treated most seriously. Your son or daughter will be reading books which contain disturbing photographs from the concentration camps maintained during that historical period. Your son or daughter will be reading actual accounts and hearing from those people who were involved in the Holocaust. Activities will be assigned which are designed to stimulate all students to think about the atrocities that occurred during the Holocaust and to become strong advocates for never allowing such things to happen again. As the philosopher George Santayana once said, "Those who cannot remember the past are condemned to repeat it."

Please feel free to participate in any of our classroom activities and discussions. Stop by or call me if you have any questions, suggestions, or concerns about this unit of study. Finally, I would like to invite you to come and participate in the "Remember the Holocaust Day" on_____, which our class will organize as a culmination to the study of the Holocaust.

Sincerely,

Holocaust Time Line

Directions: Using the information provided on page 132 of *Daniel's Story*, complete the following time line, identifying the most significant historical events. The first is listed for you.

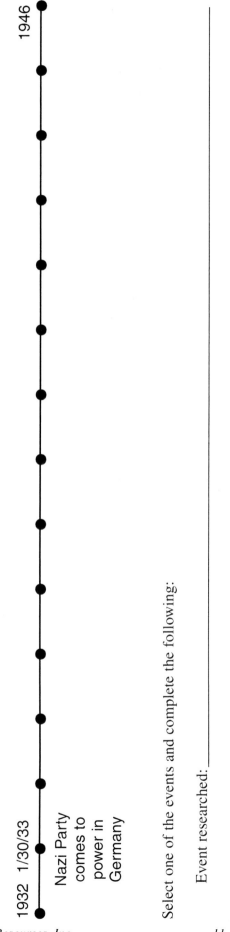

1932 1/30/33

Nazi Party
comes to
power in
Germany

1946

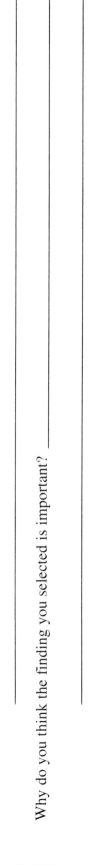

Select one of the events and complete the following:

Event researched: _____

Source(s) of information: _____

Most important finding: _____

Why do you think the finding you selected is important? _____

How did this event change the course of history? _____

Holocaust Crossword Puzzle

Directions: Use the glossary on pages 133–136 of *Daniel's Story* and complete the Holocaust Crossword Puzzle below.

Across

1. largest concentration camp
4. laws which excluded Jews socially and politically from Germany
8. underground organization engaged in struggle for liberation
9. alliance of Germany, Italy, and Japan
11. countries that opposed Germany, Italy, and Japan
12. Jewish house of worship
13. Nazi camps where inmates were forced to work
14. organized massacre of Jews
15. founder of the Nazi Party

Down

2. Nazi political police ovens used to burn bodies
3. race the Nazis believed was superior
5. ceremony inducting Jewish boys into adulthood on their thirteenth birthdays
6. restricted area of a city where Jews were required to live
7. Night of Broken Glass when Nazis burned, looted, and vandalized Jewish homes, schools, and businesses
10. abbreviation of the Nazi Secret State Police

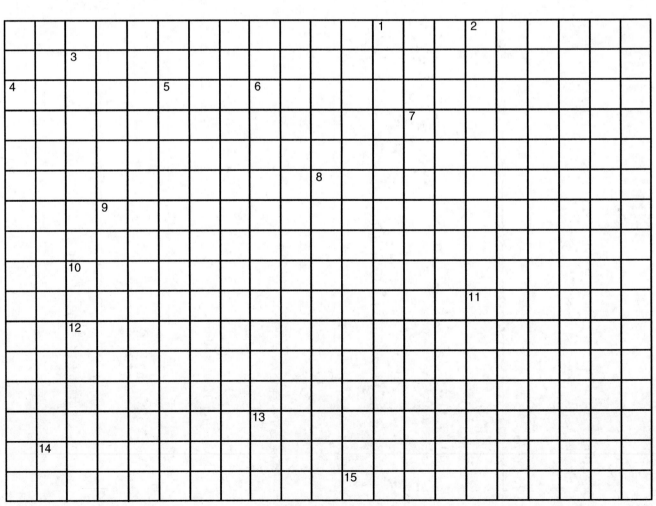

Pack Your Bags

Directions: Pretend you are forced to leave your home and you can take only items that will fit into a backpack. Make a list of what you would take.

_____   _____

_____   _____

_____   _____

_____   _____

_____   _____

_____   _____

_____   _____

_____   _____

_____   _____

Now put a number 1 in front of the item that is most important to you, a number 2 by the item of second importance, and so forth.

Explain why the item you selected as number 1 is so important to you._____

_____

_____

_____

Daniel finally had all his belongings taken from him. How would you deal with having all the things you have listed above taken from you?

_____

_____

_____

_____

Character Emotions

Directions: Think about the different emotions that Daniel and the other characters in *Daniel's Story* feel. Beside each of the feelings, list a character who felt that emotion and give an example that demonstrates it.

Emotion	Character	Example
1. Love		
2. Guilt		
3. Loneliness		
4. Trust		
5. Loyalty		
6. Disgust		
7. Anger		
8. Humor		

List other emotions you recognized, name the characters who experienced them, and give examples describing the events or experiences.

1. _____

2. _____

3. _____

4. _____

5. _____

An Ode to Daniel

Directions: Write an ode to honor Daniel. An ode is a poem that is written to honor something or someone and consists of more than one stanza. It uses formal language and maintains a serious tone throughout. Odes may rhyme in different ways—last words of first and third lines can rhyme, for example, or last words of the second and fourth lines can rhyme. In fact, you may wish to write an ode that does not rhyme at all. The main thing to keep in mind is that you wish to express admiration and respect for the person, event, or thing to which you dedicate the poem.

Ode to Daniel

Daniel's Story

What Do the History Books Say?

A Review of Information on the Holocaust

1. Name of book _____

2. Publisher _____

3. Publication date _____

4. Number of pages about the Holocaust _____

5. List of topics presented which are related to the Holocaust:

   _____   _____
   _____   _____
   _____   _____
   _____   _____

6. List of maps, graphs, charts, etc., which are presented:

   _____   _____
   _____   _____
   _____   _____
   _____   _____

7. How would you rate the Holocaust information provided?

   ____ insufficient   ____ sufficient   ____ more than sufficient

8. What might be added?_____

   _____

   _____

9. Overall summary of information provided:_____

   _____

   _____

   _____

   _____

Holocaust Events

Directions: Many important events took place in *Daniel's Story*. Select the six events that you feel are the most significant and list them below in the order in which they happened.

Event 1 _____

_____

Event 2 _____

_____

Event 3 _____

_____

Event 4 _____

_____

Event 5 _____

_____

Event 6 _____

_____

Of these events, which do you think is the . . .

saddest? _____   least believable? _____

happiest? _____   most believable? _____

strangest? _____   most informative? _____

Would you have liked to have been involved in any of these events? _____

If so, which one? _____

If not, why not? _____

Anne Frank: Beyond the Diary

by Ruud van der Rol and Rian Verhoeven

(Penguin Books, 1993)

Summary

This book provides insight into the massive upheaval which tore apart Anne Frank's world. We are shown glimpses of her life before the family went into hiding and get some idea of the influences that formed her strong moral beliefs. We learn of her early childhood, the wretched conditions of the last years of her life, and even hear testimony of the last persons to see her alive in the Bergen-Belsen concentration camp. The book does this through the use of photographs, maps, illustrations, interviews, historical essays, and most importantly, excerpts from the diary Anne Frank kept while in hiding in the Annex Building.

The outline below is a suggested plan for the activities presented in this unit. You should adapt these to your own classroom situation. Before reading *Anne Frank: Beyond the Diary* and initiating the activities, you may want to order some of the following materials from the Anti-Defamation League of B'nai B'rith, 823 United Nations Plaza, New York, NY 10017 (212) 490-2525:

Curriculum Guide—*End of Innocence: Anne Frank and the Holocaust* by Karen Shawn

Videos—*Anne Frank in Maine* (28 minutes)   *Life of Anne Frank* (30 minutes)
          Just a Diary (30 minutes)   *World of Anne Frank* (28 minutes)

Sample Plan

Lesson I

❑ Read pages 3–36.
❑ Introduce other books relating to Anne Frank's diary (see Setting the Stage, page 19, activity 1). Other materials may be secured from the Anne Frank Institue of Philadelphia (see Resource Materials, page 79).
❑ Discuss the Introduction to *Anne Frank: Beyond the Diary* (see Setting the Stage, page 19, activity 2). Note that Anna Quindlen was just about Anne Frank's age when she first read the diary.
❑ Show the video *Dear Kitty* (see Setting the Stage, page 19, activity 3).
❑ Discuss these elements in this section of the book:
-the birthday present
-the move from Frankfurt to Amsterdam
-the map showing where Anne lived during her brief life (pages 12 and 13)
-the segment on Hitler coming to power
-fleeing to another country
-German occupation of the Netherlands

Lesson II

❑ Read pages 37–86.
❑ Discuss anti-Jewish laws and assign page 21.
❑ Discuss the photographs in *Anne Frank: Beyond the Diary* (see Enjoying the Book, page 19, activity 2).
❑ Discuss these elements in this section of the book:
-Dear Kitty
-actual pictures of Anne's diary and house
-deportation of Jews
-street map of Amsterdam (with canals)
-sister Margot and cutaway view of the house
-going into hiding

Lesson III

❑ Read pages 87–107.
❑ Assign students to illustrate rooms in hiding on page 22.
❑ Discuss the purposes of an obituary, a eulogy, and an epitaph and then ask students to create one of each for Anne Frank on page 25.
❑ Discuss other Holocaust victims in hiding (see Extending the Book, page 20, activity 3).
❑ Discuss these elements in this section of the book:
-the diary is left behind
-pictures from the concentration camps
-map of major concentration camps (pages 91 and 95), containing information on estimated number of Jews killed in various countries during the war

Lesson IV

❑ Discuss the quotation from Anne Frank's diary that appears on page 106 of the book: *You've known for a long time that my greatest wish is to become . . . a famous writer.* (May ll, 1944)
-How has her wish come true?
-Why is this considered ironic?
-Would her wish have come true if she had lived? Why?
❑ Assign students to create diary entries for Anne Frank on page 23.
❑ Assign students to complete the character analysis on page 24.
❑ Assign students to create a poster on page 26 for an Anne Frank presentation.

Overview of Activities

Setting the Stage

1. Read page 110 of *Anne Frank: Beyond the Diary*, which will tell the students about the different versions of the diary of Anne Frank that are available. As indicated, the first diary that was published in the United States was in 1952, entitled *Anne Frank: The Diary of a Young Girl*. Obtain a copy of this book along with copies of the books related to Anne Frank. Encourage the students to read as many of these books as possible and then allow time to discuss what they have learned about Anne Frank and the Holocaust.

2. Anna Quindlen, a well-known columnist, wrote the Introduction to *Anne Frank: Beyond the Diary*. Read the "Introduction" orally to the students and discuss how it makes them feel—not only about Anne Frank's life but about their own lives as well. Discuss how everyone goes about the day-to-day business of life no matter what their lives demand. Most people, including Anne Frank, know little about the inner thoughts and feeling of others. Reading such a document enables all of us to understand that we are like others—not alone or unusual or peculiar but human beings with real feelings which deserve honor and respect. Ask your students to return to this section after reading this book and then to write their own introductions.

3. For free and inexpensive materials on this theme, write to the following address:

   The Anne Frank Center
   106 East 19th Street
   New York, NY 10003
   (212) 529-9532

   Also, the the Anne Frank Center has available a video, *Dear Kitty*, which tells the life of Anne Frank. It would be most interesting for your students to see.

Enjoying the Book

1. Discuss the various Jewish laws that Anne Frank wrote about in her diary. (For example, Jews had to wear a yellow star, Jews had to hand in their bicycles, Jews were banned from trains and were forbidden to use any car, etc.) Then ask the students to think about how laws such as these would affect them if they were imposed today. Complete the activity on page 21.

2. Allow time for the students to look at the pictures of Anne and her family which appear in *Anne Frank: Beyond the Diary*. Then discuss what the students found out about Anne, her family, and the kind of life they had prior to the time they were sent off to concentration camps.

3. Although there is a diagram showing Anne Frank's room in the Annex, ask the students to complete the activity on page 22 by illustrating in detail how they think Anne's room in the Annex looked and how their room would look if they were forced into a similar situation.

4. Anne Frank did not continue her diary after she was captured by the Germans. Tell the students to pretend to be Anne and to write entries for five days into a diary on page 23. Reproduce additional pages for those who need them.

Overview of Activities *(cont.)*

Extending the Book

1. Ask the students to do a character analysis of the people who were in *Anne Frank: Beyond the Diary* by completing the activity on page 24. By its nature, the matrix shown here admits only a simple check for each characteristic and does not really explore each person's character. Some of these individuals appearing in the book are more fully developed than others. After completing the activity, engage the students in discussion about the most interesting characters. Is it possible for one character to display contradictory characteristics? Why? When?

2. When someone dies, a death notice (an obituary) is usually published and a eulogy or speech honoring the person is often delivered at the funeral. In addition, many people have an inscription or epitaph written on their tombstones. Discuss and explain these traditions with the class. Ask the students to collect some obituaries from the newspapers and some eulogies, if possible. Also, visit a nearby cemetery to look at the various inscriptions on tombstones. Then ask the students to complete the activity on page 25.

3. There are other books available, such as *The Room Upstairs* by Johanna Reiss or *The Hidden Children: The Secret Survivors of the Holocaust* by Jane Marks, which tell about people who tried to escape the Nazis by hiding in closets, attics, etc. Obtain copies of these books for the students to read and then compare them with Anne Frank's ordeal. Discuss what the reasons might be for Anne Frank becoming so famous when there were many others like her.

4. Discuss with the students the following hypothetical situation: If Anne Frank were alive today and coming to speak to their school or community, what do they think her message would be? Ask the students to create on page 26 a poster advertising her presentation.

5. Survey the literature-related activities on pages 55 and 56 for annotated suggestions about other books related to Anne Frank's ordeal during the Holocaust. Some of the titles are as follows:

   * *Number the Stars* by Lois Lowry, Houghton Mifflin, 1989
   * *I Never Saw Another Butterfly* by Hana Volavkova, Schocken, 1993
   * *Alicia: My Story* by Alicia Appleman-Jurman, Bantam, 1988
   * *The Devil's Arithmetic* by Jan Yolen, Viking, 1988

   The brief summaries and suggested activities will prove effective in planning additional reading and related ways to extend the book.

6. Supplementary activities on page 68 will also serve as strong extenders for *Anne Frank: Beyond the Diary*. Among these are suggestions about the film *Schindler's List*, making a Holocaust collage, inviting living witnesses, investigating antagonistic groups, creating a campaign to stamp out prejudice, investigating the history of persecution, learning about Jewish holidays, and studying famous statements about the Holocaust.

Anti-Jewish Laws

Directions: The Nazis passed and implemented many anti-Jewish laws such as these—Jews may use only Jewish barbers; Jews must be indoors from 8:00 P.M. to 6:00 A.M., etc. List at least six of these laws you have read about, pretend these laws were passed against your culture, and explain how the enforcement of such laws would change your life.

Law 1 _____

_____

How would this law change your life?_____

_____

Law 2 _____

_____

_____

How would this law change your life?_____

_____

Law 3 _____

_____

How would this law change your life?_____

_____

Law 4 _____

_____

How would this law change your life?_____

_____

Law 5 _____

_____

How would this law change your life?_____

_____

Law 6 _____

_____

How would this law change your life?_____

_____

Room in Hiding

Directions: On the top part of this page, make an illustration of Anne's room in the Annex. On the bottom half of the page illustrate what your room would look like if you were forced into hiding.

Anne's Room in the Annex

My Room in Hiding

A Diary

Directions: After she was captured, of course, Anne was unable to continue writing in her diary. Select five days of Anne Frank's life after her capture by the Nazis and write a diary entry for her for each of those five days. Enter the month and year of your entry.

Diary—After the Capture

Month_____   Year_____

Character Analysis

Directions: Below is a list of characters in *Anne Frank: Beyond the Diary*. Place a check mark in each box that accurately describes the character.

Character	Heroic	Brave	Evil	Good	Sweet	Mischievous	Friendly	Caring	Loving	Energetic	Optimistic	Pessimistic	Intelligent	Selfish
Anne Frank														
Margot Frank														
Otto Frank														
Edith Frank														
Grandmother Hollander														
Adolf Hitler														
Miep Gies														
Jan Gies														
Hermann Van Pels														
Peter Van Pels														
Mrs. Van Pels														
Bep Voskuijl														
Victor Kugler														
Johannes Kleiman														

Select the character who interested you the most. In the space provided below and on the back of this page, write a brief essay telling why you selected the character.

I feel I was most interested in_____because _____

_____

_____

_____

_____

Anne's Obituary, Eulogy, and Epitaph

Directions: Anne Frank died when she was a prisoner in Bergen-Belsen. In the spaces provided below, write an obituary, a eulogy, and an epitaph for Anne Frank. (An *obituary* is a notice of a person's death appearing in a newspaper. It often contains a summary of the life, work, and accomplishments of the person. It is written in a factual, objective manner. A *eulogy* is a speech or essay given in praise and admiration for a person after that person's death. It is warm and admiring in tone. An *epitaph* is a brief inscription appearing on a person's tombstone. It is usually warm in tone and often philosophical in nature.

Anne Frank—An Obituary

Anne Frank—A Eulogy

Anne Frank—An Epitaph

Anne Frank's Presentation

Directions: Pretend Anne Frank is alive and that she is coming to make a presentation at your school. Think about what her message would be and then create a poster advertising her presentation.

Elie Wiesel: Voice From the Holocaust

by Michael A. Schuman
(Enslow Publishing, Inc., 1994)

Summary

During World War II, Elie Wiesel, then 15 years of age, and his family were taken from their home and forced into Nazi concentration camps. Only Wiesel and two of his sisters survived. Elie became determined that a tragedy such as the Holocaust should never be allowed to happen again. Therefore, he has dedicated his life to keeping the memory of the Holocaust alive through his writings and speaking. He was the recipient of the Nobel Peace Prize in 1986. This book tells about his extraordinary life.

The outline below is a suggested plan for using the various activities presented in this unit. You should adapt these to fit your own classroom situation.

Sample Plan

Lesson I

❏ Begin reading *Elie Wiesel: Voice From the Holocaust* (Chapters 1–4).
❏ Discuss Chapter 1 (see page 28, Setting the Stage, activity 1).
❏ Discuss the following topics from Chapters 2–4:
  -Wiesel's studious boyhood and special feeling for his grandfather
  -the seeds of WW II—blame for WW I defeat, the economy, inflation, and unemployment
  -Hitler becomes Chancellor in 1933, anti-Jewish feelings, immigration laws
  -annexing Austria, Czechoslovakia
  -persistent beliefs of Jews that persecution could not really exist
  -capture, internment, tattoos

Lesson II

❏ Continue reading *Elie Wiesel: Voice From the Holocaust* (Chapters 5–7).
❏ Discuss the Nobel Peace Prize and assign page 31.
❏ Research Wiesel and Ossietzky's works (see page 28, Setting the Stage, activity 4).
❏ Discuss the following topics from Chapters 5–7:
  -leaving for France after liberation at age 16
  -hearing word of sisters Hilda and Beatrice
  -enrollment at the Sorbonne in Paris
  -becoming a journalist, learning English
  -silence about the camps—inability to speak of them for 10 years
  -important meeting with Francois Mauriac
  -publication of *La Nuit*, Mauriac writes the foreword
  -revisiting Germany
  -metaphor of the watch he received at his bar mitzvah

Lesson III

❏ Continue reading *Elie Wiesel: Voice From the Holocaust* (Chapters 8–9).
❏ Extend reading about Elie Wiesel (see page 28, Setting the Stage, activity 2).
❏ Discuss negative/positive happenings in Elie Wiesel's life. Assign the activity on page 30.
❏ Assign the students to develop vocabulary related to Jewish culture by completing the activity on page 32.
❏ Discus the following topics in Chapters 8–9:
  -Wiesel's career as a teacher at CUNY and Boston University
  -his first child being born in 1972
  -the image of bystanders watching cattle car roundups of people
  -the revisionists—denials of the Holocaust
  -President Carter's Holocaust Memorial Council
  -museum, library, and Day of Remembrance— April 24, 1979
  -"Memory may be our only answer."
  -Congressional Medal of Achievement from President Reagan, 1985
  -Wiesel's message to young people, page 100

Lesson IV

❏ Ask the students to review the events in the activity on page 33 and then make predictions.
❏ Ask the students to create an interview for Elie Wiesel in the activity on page 34.
❏ Create the Situation Cards game on page 35. For directions, see page 29, Extending the Book, activity 2.

Overview of Activities

Setting the Stage

1. Read Chapter 1—"Nobel Laureate"—orally to the students. Then ask such questions as the following:

   • What do the students know about the Holocaust?

   • Are the students familiar with Elie Wiesel and any of his works?

   • What kind of impact can a person such as Elie Wiesel have on the future?

   • What is the meaning of the passage from his acceptance speech on page 10?

   • In general, what reaction do the students have to this chapter?

2. Make available as many books written by Elie Wiesel as possible—for example, *Night* (1968), *Daron* (1961), *The Accident* (1961), *The Jews of Silence* (1966), *A Beggar in Jerusalem* (1970), *The Forgotten* (1992). Divide the students into groups and assign each group a book to read. After sufficient time has been given to read the books, allow time for the groups to meet and plan a creative way to present the books to the class. Then have each group present its selection.

3. Discuss with the students the fact that although there were many negative happenings in Elie Wiesel's life, there were also many positive happenings. Discuss whether this is true for most people. Ask the students to complete the activity on page 30.

4. Elie Wiesel won the Nobel Peace Prize in 1986. Explain that Nobel Prizes are given each year to pay tribute to men and women whose achievements have benefited people around the world. Point out that page 11 of *Elie Wiesel: Voice From the Holocaust* states that exactly 50 years earlier (1936) the Nobel Peace Prize was awarded to a German pacifist, Carl von Ossietzky, who tried to warn people about the growing strength of the Nazi Party and the threat to peace it represented. Ask the students to research Wiesel and Ossietzky's works that won them the Nobel Peace Prizes and to be prepared to discuss the relationship between the two.

5. Ask the students to research the Nobel Peace Prize and complete the activity on page 31.

6. Elie Wiesel became a prolific writer of both fact and fiction. Literature has become a major field for him, using words to impress images on the mind and to prolong memory. The discipline has helped him to condense his thought and pattern his ideas. Ask students to share in this discipline by completing the "Holocaust Cinquain" activity on page 36.

7. Writers other than Wiesel have spoken eloquently of the Holocaust and tried to emphasize how important it is for all humankind never to forget the awful results of unchecked prejudice and hate. Ask students to reflect on the meanings of statements made by several of those writers, restating or paraphrasing their thoughts in the students' own words. Have them do the activities on pages 37 and 38, "Famous Quotations."

Overview of Activities *(cont.)*

Enjoying the Book

1. Discuss with the students that throughout *Elie Wiesel: Voice From the Holocaust* there are Yiddish words and terms related to the Jewish culture. Explain that Yiddish is a High German language with a mixture of vocabulary from Hebrew and Slavic. It is used mostly by Jews from central and eastern Europe and written in Hebrew letters. A number of Yiddish words have been borrowed into English and made their way into mainstream use. (For more information on Yiddish, write to National Yiddish Book Center. See page 79.) Other terms related to Jewish culture are becoming widely understood throughout the United States and other countries as the world becomes more cosmopolitan. To help students better understand Jewish culture, ask them to complete the activity on page 32.

2. Ask the students to read the events in the activity on page 33 and then make predictions. These passages reflect and recount actual occurrences, but the students are asked to suggest what might have happened if other steps had been taken—a valuable lesson in considering alternatives and an absolute necessity for the development of forethought.

3. Using concept webs to help students organize thought and remember facts and relationships is an effective technique. Ask students to do the "Create a Web" activity on page 42, using their reading from *Elie Wiesel: Voice From the Holocaust* as the topic.

Extending the Book

1. After the students have completed the activity on page 34, work as a group to compile 10 interview questions for Mr. Wiesel and to create a cover letter to him. Mail the letter and questions to Mr. Wiesel via the publisher at the following address:

   Enslow Publishers, Inc.
   Bloy Street and Ramsey Avenue
   Box 777
   Hillside, NJ 07205

2. Glue page 35 to cardboard or reproduce it on heavy cardstock. Laminate, cut the cards apart, and place them in a box. Divide the students into cooperative learning groups and tell them to select one of the situation cards. Allow 10 minutes for the group to discuss the situation presented on the card and to be prepared to lead a discussion with remaining students. The discussion can take the form of a debate, a panel discussion, or a survey of opinion with questions and answers.

3. Literary evaluation is a powerful way to help analyze and retain material we have read. Ask students to do activities on page 43, "Fact or Opinion"; page 44, "Make the Grade"; and page 46, "People of the Holocaust."

4. Retelling events one has read about is one way of strengthening memory and developing self-confidence. Ask students to do the activity on page 53, "Newscast from Berlin," which involves such retelling along with a bit of role-playing.

5. Ask students to do activities on page 60, "Avenue of the Righteous"; and page 61, "Take a Risk." One of Elie Wiesel's strongest messages is the importance of people refusing to stand by and watch injustice simply because it is happening to others—not ourselves. These activities direct our attention to that point.

Good and Bad

Directions: Elie Wiesel had many bad things as well as good things happen to him throughout his life. On the balance scale below, make a list of the good and bad happenings.

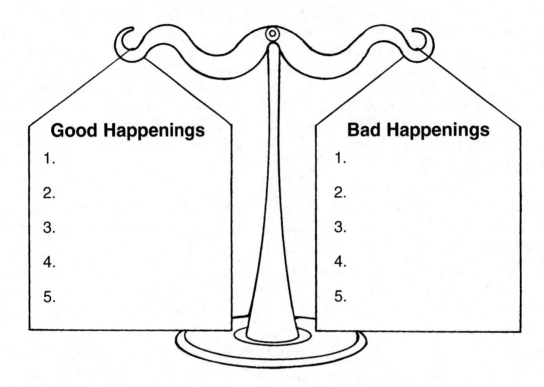

Good Happenings

1.

2.

3.

4.

5.

Bad Happenings

1.

2.

3.

4.

5.

Do you think there is a fairly even balance between the good and bad happenings in Elie Wiesel's life?_____Explain. _____

_____

_____

Do you think Elie Wiesel could have made choices in his life that would have made his life easier and better?_____Explain. _____

_____

_____

Do you think Elie Wiesel could have made choices in his life that would have made his life more difficult or worse?_____Explain. _____

_____

_____

Nobel Peace Prize

1. Explain the Nobel Peace Prize. _____
   _____
   _____

2. List the recipients of the Nobel Peace Prize for the last five years.

   Year   **Recipient**

   _____   _____

   _____   _____

   _____   _____

   _____   _____

   _____   _____

3. Select one of these recipients and describe in detail why this person received the prize. _____
   _____
   _____
   _____
   _____
   _____
   _____
   _____

4. How do you think the contribution of the recipient you reviewed above compares to the
   contribution Elie Wiesel made?_____Explain. _____
   _____
   _____
   _____

5. If you could select the recipient for this year's Nobel Peace Prize, whom would you select?
   _____Why? _____
   _____
   _____
   _____

What Is a Mensch?

Directions: Match the words and terms related to the Jewish culture on the left with the correct definitions on the right by putting the correct letter on the blank.

_____ 1. mensch

_____ 2. Talmud

_____ 3. synagogue

_____ 4. Hasidic Jews

_____ 5. Passover

_____ 6. Rosh Hashanah

_____ 7. bar mitzvah

_____ 8. cabala

_____ 9. Yom Kippur

_____ 10. Torah

a. gave own special interpretation to basic tenets of the Jewish religion

b. Jewish New Year

c. writings that form the basis of Jewish law and lore

d. commemorates the exodus of Jews out of Egypt about 3,250 years ago

e. a person of strong character

f. Jewish bible

g. a Jewish house of worship

h. Day of Atonement

i. a Jewish school of mystical thought

j. a ceremony that takes place at age 13, marking the transition from boyhood to manhood

Predictions

Directions: Below are events from *Elie Wiesel: Voice From the Holocaust*. Read each event and predict what might have happened if the event were changed. Remember, a prediction is what one believes will happen; there are no right or wrong answers.

1. In 1940, early in the period of World War II, Elie's father, Shlomo, was arrested and jailed for two months because he was secretly helping Jews escape from Nazi-occupied Poland. Shortly after Shlomo was released from prison and returned home, Elie's mother, Sarah, considered moving Elie's family to Palestine which was seen as a haven for oppressed Jews. But Elie's father felt such a move was unnecessary, and they did not move. Predict how Elie's life would have been different if they had moved to Palestine in 1940.

Predictions

_____

_____

_____

2. On December 7, 1941, the Japanese bombed the U.S. Naval Base at Pearl Harbor in Hawaii, and on December 8, President Franklin D. Roosevelt declared war on Japan. Three days later Germany declared war on the United States. American people had been split on whether or not the U.S. should be involved in the war in Europe. Predict how the course of history might have been different if the U.S. had not become involved in the war in Europe.

Predictions

_____

_____

_____

3. In 1942, Wiesel's friend Moshe was taken away with others on crowded railroad cars. After several months, Moshe escaped and returned to Sighet (the town where Elie lived) and told horrible stories about the mass murders. He told about how Jewish people were being forced to dig their own graves, after which they were shot. Stories such as Moshe told were being rumored throughout the Jewish communities of Europe. Nobody believed these stories and simply thought it was typical war propaganda. Predict how events of the Holocaust might be different if the Jewish people had actually known and believed what was going on.

Predictions

_____

_____

_____

Elie Wiesel's Interview

Directions: Create 10 interview questions that you would ask Elie Wiesel if you were interviewing him. Some areas of interest to consider for questioning might be these:

- curbing organized crime (gangs and how they might relate to the brutality of the Holocaust)
- keeping memories alive after the deaths of those who experienced the Holocaust
- recognizing dangerous trends in today's societies
- using education as a guard against future holocausts

1. _____
   _____

2. _____
   _____

3. _____
   _____

4. _____
   _____

5. _____
   _____

6. _____
   _____

7. _____
   _____

8. _____
   _____

9. _____
   _____

10. _____
    _____

Which three of these questions do you feel are the most important?_____

Why?_____

_____

_____

Situation Cards

There are groups of people who maintain the Holocaust never happened. What do you think?	When he visited Europe in the 1960s and 1970s, Elie Wiesel believed that most German people were ignoring the fact that the Holocaust ever happened. What do you think Germans today should do in response to the Holocaust?
There has been a reaction by some who say that Elie Wiesel has not spoken up for other groups of people who aren't Jewish and yet are being oppressed. What do you think?	There are neo-Nazi groups (people who support Hitler's ideas) existing in Germany and other countries today. How do you feel the governments of these countries should deal with these groups?
There are some people who believe that Elie Wiesel has capitalized on his unfortunate experiences as a Holocaust victim. They believe he is more interested in his own publicity and financial benefits than the causes he champions. What do you think?	The Wiesels have sponsored conferences around the world on a variety of topics. A recent topic at these conferences has been the analysis of hate—why people hate and how hate can be controlled. What do you think should be done to control hate?
Elie Wiesel believes it is important to make every effort possible to inform people about the Holocaust—e.g., by establishing Holocaust Museums in Washington, D.C., and other locations. A common saying attributed to the Spanish philosopher George Santayana states that "He who does not remember history is bound to repeat it." What do you think?	Elie Wiesel has received many awards and prizes, including the coveted Noble Peace Prize. After reading *Elie Wiesel: Voice From the Holocaust*, do you believe he is worthy of all this recognition? Explain.

Holocaust Cinquain

Directions: Write a cinquain poem about the Holocaust. A cinquain consists of the following:

Cinquain Poetry Form	**Sample Cinquain**
Line 1: One word (It may be a title.)	Holocaust
Line 2: Two words (These describe the title.)	Terrible massacre
Line 3: Three words (These express an action.)	Nazis killing millions
Line 4: Four Words (These express a feeling.)	Fear, terror, horror, hostility
Line 5: One word (This refers to the title.)	Murder

_____

_____

_____

_____

_____

Illustrate your poem or design a border for it:

Famous Quotations

Directions: Following are statements made by various observers, victims, and students of the Holocaust. On the lines following each quotation, try to paraphrase—that is, restate in your own words—or otherwise express what you think these people are trying to tell the world about the seriousness of these events in our history.

1. *"How do you describe the sorting out on arriving at Auschwitz, the separation of children who see a father or mother going away, never to be seen again? How do you express the dumb grief of a little girl and the endless lines of women, children, and rabbis being driven across the Polish or Ukrainian landscapes to their deaths? No, I can't do it. And because I'm a writer and teacher, I don't understand how Europe's most cultured nation could have done that. So what happened?"*

—Elie Wiesel

_____

_____

_____

_____

2. *"For the dead and the living we must bear witness."*

—Elie Wiesel

_____

_____

_____

_____

3. *"The concentration camps, by making death itself anonymous (making it impossible to find out whether a prisoner is dead or alive), robbed death of its meaning as the end of a fulfilled life. In a sense they took away the individual's own death, proving that henceforth nothing belonged to him and he belonged to no one. His death merely set a seal on the fact that he had never existed."*

—Hannah Arendt

(German-born U.S. political philosopher. *The Origins of Totalitarianism*, 1951.)

_____

_____

_____

_____

Famous Quotations *(cont.)*

Directions: Following are statements made by various observers, victims, and students of the Holocaust. On the lines following each quotation, try to paraphrase—that is, restate in your own words—or otherwise express what you think these people are trying to tell the world about the seriousness of these events in our history.

4. *"Despite the hundreds of attempts, police terror and the concentration camps have proved to be more or less impossible subjects for the artist; since what happened to them was beyond the imagination, it was therefore also beyond art and all those human values on which art is traditionally based."*

—A. Alvarez

(British critic, poet, and novelist. *The Savage God*, 1971.)

_____

_____

_____

_____

5. *"If you complain of people being shot down in the streets, of the absence of communication or social responsibility, of the rise of everyday violence which people have become accustomed to, and the dehumanization of feelings, then the ultimate development on an organized social level is the concentration camp . . . . The concentration camp is the final expression of human separateness and its ultimate consequence. It is organized abandonment.*

—Arthur Miller

(U.S. dramatist. *Paris Review,* Summer 1966.)

_____

_____

_____

_____

6. *"The things I saw beggar description . . . . The visual evidence and the verbal testimony of starvation, cruelty, and bestiality were so overpowering . . . . I made the visit deliberately, in order to be in a position to give firsthand evidence of these things if ever, in the future, there develops a tendency to charge these allegations to propaganda."*

—Dwight D. Eisenhower

(U.S. General and President of the United States. These words are carved into the wall at the entrance of the United States Holocaust Memorial Museum in Washington, D.C.)

_____

_____

_____

Dear Mr. President

Directions: Adolf Hitler was appointed Chancellor of Germany in 1933. After that time, Jews, Gypsies, homosexuals, handicapped people, and others became the prime targets for persecution. During his dictatorship from 1933–1945, nearly 6,000,000 Jews were murdered. Pretend you were alive in 1940 and know what you know today. Write the president of the United States a letter about what you think his country should do.

_____

_____

_____

Dear Mr. President:

Pretend

1. Pretend you are Jewish, living in Germany in 1943, and you capture a German soldier.
   What would you do? _____

   _____

   Whom would your actions affect? _____

   What would the effects be?_____

2. Pretend you are a Jewish parent of a ten-year-old daughter and an eight-year-old daughter. The Germans tell you that you can take only one child with you, and the other must go with them.
   What would you do? _____

   _____

   Whom would your actions affect? _____

   What would the effects be?_____

3. Pretend you, your family, and other Jewish neighbors have little to eat and that every time the Germans give you a loaf of bread, it is divided evenly among everyone. One day, you find a box of canned food that is packed away.
   What would you do? _____

   Whom would your actions affect? _____

   What would the effects be?_____

4. Pretend you are Jewish, you own your own business, and the Nuremberg Laws are issued in which the Jews are excluded from German social and political life. Many of your friends and relatives are beginning to move to other countries.
   What would you do? _____

   Whom would your actions affect? _____

   What would the effects be?_____

5. Almost daily the news media around the world report accounts of people or groups of people who are suffering from prejudice and injustices—for example, the people of Bosnia.
   What can you do to help eliminate prejudice? _____

   _____

   Whom would your actions affect? _____

   What would the effects be?_____

Crack the Code

Directions: Read each sentence. Circle the code letter below to show whether the sentence is true or false. For example, the first statement is false. Therefore, under statement 1 in the chart below the sentences, you would circle the letter "O."

1. The word *holocaust* means "sacred cause."

2. Adolf Hitler was the Chancellor of Germany during the period of the Holocaust.

3. *Kristallnacht* is a German word meaning the "Night of Broken Glass."

4. Germans kept the Jews in concentration camps and treated them well.

5. The Germans murdered only women and men.

6. *Nazi* is an acronym for National Socialist German Workers Party.

7. Hitler was admired and respected by all German people.

8. An estimated 6,000,000 Jewish people died during the Holocaust period.

9. Anne Frank survived the Holocaust.

10. The Nazi murders included thousands of non-Jews such as Gypsies, the handicapped, and homosexuals.

11. The concept of anti-Semitism—prejudice against Jewish cultural/religious differences—began with the Holocaust.

12. The economy was good in Germany when Hitler began his dictatorship.

13. The Nuremberg Laws forbade marriages between Jews and Germans.

14. Denmark assisted in getting some Jews to safety.

Statement	1	2	3	4	5	6	7	8	9	10	11	12	13	14	
True	P	E	M	S	A	D	K	N	X	O	R	W	E	O	
False	O	Q	T	I	N	L	R	U	G	V	E	C	K	C	

Write the circled letters in the blanks below to find out an important message concerning the Holocaust. For example, the first statement is false, and therefore the letter "O" is circled and the letter "O" is written above the numeral 1.

___ ___   ___ ___ ___ ___   ___ ___ ___ ___ ___ ___ ___ ___
5   1   3   14   7   2   9   13   8   10   12   4   6   11

Create a Web

Directions: A web or a semantic map is a way of organizing or outlining information about a topic. For example, if you create a web or semantic map for the word *curious*, it might look something like this:

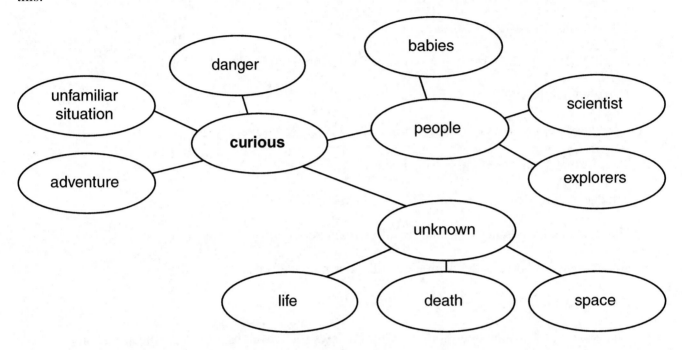

Create a web/semantic map using the word "Holocaust." You will need to think about all the key words associated with Holocaust. Compare your mapping with that of other students in the class.

Fact or Opinion

Directions: A fact is something that can be proven to be true. For example, "The grass is green" is a fact. An opinion is something that cannot be proven true. For example, "John's hair is too long" is an opinion. Read the following statements about the Holocaust. Put an F in the blank if the statement is a fact. Put an O in the blank if the statement is an opinion.

_____ 1. Adolf Hitler was appointed as Chancellor of Germany.

_____ 2. All Germans hated the Jews.

_____ 3. The Jewish people should have left Europe.

_____ 4. Many Jews were murdered during the Holocaust.

_____ 5. Laws were passed that deprived Jews of German citizenship.

_____ 6. Jews did not realize what was happening to them.

_____ 7. Jewish shops and businesses were burned, looted, and destroyed.

_____ 8. The Nazi Party was proclaimed by law to be the only legal political party in Germany.

_____ 9. If Jewish people had cooperated with Hitler and his Nazi Party, they would not have been killed.

_____ 10. Concentration camps were established for the Jews.

_____ 11. Other countries should have done more to help save the Jewish people.

_____ 12. German officers were adequately punished for what they did to the Jewish people.

_____ 13. American troops joined other countries in trying to stop the German aggression and atrocities against Jews.

_____ 14. All Jews in German occupied areas were required to wear the yellow Star of David.

_____ 15. Hitler committed suicide.

Make the Grade

Directions: Specific literary elements (characterization, plot, theme, setting, point of view) are used to develop a story. The way these elements are developed makes the difference between a good piece of literature and a weak piece of literature. The following explanation of literary elements can help you evaluate the books you read.

Characterization: This term refers to the methods by which characters are developed. Characters are revealed through conversation, actions, and behaviors; through narration; and through comments of others.

Plot: This term refers to the story line, the happenings that keep the reader involved and interested in the book.

Theme: This term refers to the message or feeling that the author is trying to convey.

Setting: This term refers to the where and the when of the story. The setting transports the reader to the time and the place of the story.

Point of View: This term refers to the person through whose eyes the story unfolds. The story may be told in first person (I) or in third person (he, she, or they).

Select one book you have read related to the Holocaust. Using the following grading scale, grade each literary element for that book and *provide explanations* (using examples from the book) of why you assigned the grades you did.

Grade Scale

A = excellent
B = good
C = fair
D = not very good
F = not good

_____
Title of Book

_____
Author

Literary Element	Grade	Explanation
Characterization		
Plot		
Theme		
Setting		
Point of View		

Good Traits and Bad Traits

Directions: People have traits that are considered good and traits that are considered bad. Make a list of traits that you would consider good—for example, honesty and sympathy. Then make a list of traits that you would consider bad—for example, deceit and cruelty.

Good Traits	Bad Traits
_____	_____
_____	_____
_____	_____

Select one of the books you have read that is related to the Holocaust. Name three characters from that book who have good traits and three characters who have bad traits. In addition, list the most significant good or bad traits for each.

Book Title: _____ **Author:** _____

Characters with Good Traits   Most Significant Good Traits

1. _____   _____
2. _____   _____
3. _____   _____

Characters with Bad Traits   Most Significant Bad Traits

1. _____   _____
2. _____   _____
3. _____   _____

Directions: Name three of your best friends and identify one good trait for each.

Names of Friends	Good Traits
1. _____	1. _____
2. _____	2. _____
3. _____	3. _____

People of the Holocaust

Directions: List five different people you have read about during the study of the Holocaust.

Character	Title of Book	Author
1.		
2.		
3.		
4.		
5.		

If you could meet one of the characters listed above, who would it be?

_____

Why?_____

What five questions would you like to ask the person you selected?

1. _____

2. _____

3. _____

4. _____

5. _____

What answers do you think you would receive?

1. _____

2. _____

3. _____

4. _____

5. _____

The ABC's of the Holocaust

Directions: Along the side of this page are the 26 letters of the alphabet. For each letter, write a word or phrase which begins with that letter and relates to the Holocaust. In the right-hand column, fill in a brief definition or explanation of the word or phrase written in the left-hand column. The first two are done for you. See how many words or phrases you can accumulate to complete the alphabet.

	Word/Phrases	Definition/Explanation
A	anti-Semitism	being prejudiced against Jews
B	Buchenwald	concentration camp in Germany
C		
D		
E		
F		
G		
H		
I		
J		
K		
L		
M		
N		
O		
P		
Q		
R		
S		
T		
U		
V		
W		
X		
Y		
Z		

Name the Character

Directions: After reading Holocaust-related books such as *Daniel's Story* by Carol Matas, *Anne Frank: Beyond the Diary* by Ruud van der Rol and Rian Verhoeven, or *Elie Wiesel: Voice From the Holocaust* by Michael A. Schuman, complete the following by listing a character or characters in the center column who would fit the description in the right column.

Book	Character	Description
		heroic
		unusual
		cruel
		strong
		kind
		frightened
		intelligent
		selfish
		courageous
		cowardly

Which of these characters would you like best as a friend?

_____

Why?_____

_____

Create a Story

Use heavy cardstock to reproduce the cards on pages 50–52. Laminate the cards and cut them apart. Separate all cards marked C (for *character*), P (for *plot* or *problem*), S (for *setting*), and CON (for *conclusion*) and place them in four separate containers. Divide the students into groups of four and tell them to number themselves 1, 2, 3, and 4. All "ones" draw a character (C) card, all "twos" a plot (P) card, all "threes" a setting (S) card, and all "fours" a conclusion (CON) card.

Allow each group of four to work as a cooperative group to create a story involving the character, plot, setting, and conclusion cards they drew. The story should be a complete episode or series of episodes with a beginning, middle, and end. After sufficient preparation time, the students should read, present, or dramatize their stories for the entire class. (This activity can be used to produce multimedia presentations if computers and software are available to the classroom. The addition of music, sound, graphics, and quoted text can help blend fictional and nonfictional elements into a genuinely creative production.)

At the beginning of this presentation, the students should explain which cards they drew so the audience can appreciate how the group used the information they were provided. Have them display their cards, announce the title of their story, and then begin the presentation. Following are some possibilities for different ways to present the group productions.

Possible Modes of Presentation

- Reproduced copies of the short story written and edited by the group

- Oral readings of the short story by one member of the group

- Readers' theater presentations of the story

- Narrative poems composed around the theme and events of the story

- Short plays depicting events in the story

- Short pantomimes depicting events in the story

- Pictorial panels depicting events in the story, accompanied by narration

- TV scripts (news stories with anchor and contributing reporters, documentary style with narration, or drama with actors) and production

- Diary entries by one or two characters, depicting events in the story

- Multimedia presentations using narration, dialog, sound, text, graphics, and music

---

Create a Story *(cont.)*

a young Jewish boy C	a German soldier C
a lonely child C	a starving man C
Adolf Hitler C	an old, thin, weak-looking woman C
an inmate C	a prisoner in chains C
a man with a gun C	a corpse C
a concentration camp S	a gas chamber S

Create a Story *(cont.)*

a boxcar train S	a crowded room of people S
a Jewish-owned store S	a Jewish ghetto S
a synagogue S	Poland in 1939 S
an open pit S	a death camp S
Trains are crowded with people. P	Laws are passed that make Jews second-class citizens. P
Books are being burned. P	Searches are conducted to find all Jews. P

Create a Story *(cont.)*

Pogroms are occurring in which Jewish businesses are trashed and Jews are being killed. P	Jewish people are being gassed and cremated. P
Cruel medical experiments are being conducted. P	Some Jews are forming resistance groups to fight the Germans. P
Many people die of starvation. CON	Germans are defeated. CON
Much of Jewish culture is destroyed. CON	Survivors end up in displaced persons camp. CON
Families are separated. CON	War trials are held. CON
The state of Israel is established. CON	Many people are gassed or cremated. CON
Survivors recall the horror and pain. CON	Museums are built in memory of the millions who were murdered during the Holocaust. CON

Newscast from Berlin

Directions: You are a resistance reporter secretly broadcasting from Berlin in the 1940s. Select at least 10 of the terms in the word bank below and use them to write a newscast script for your American audience. Assume that many people may still not fully understand what many of these words signify. Weave your explanations into your account of events inside Germany and circle the words wherever you have used them. A suggested beginning for your script appears below.

When your script is complete (edited and proofread), read it to the class. If you have done a good job, your audience will understand all you have told them.

• genocide	• Holocaust	• crematorium
• ghetto	• anti-Semitism	• Auschwitz
• resistance	• Kristallnacht	• Kapo
• Hitler	• Nazi	• pogroms
• Aryan	• Gestapo	• swastika

Good evening, Ladies and Gentlemen of the outside world. This is_____broadcasting from a secret location inside Berlin, Germany, on June____, 194___. I have only a brief time on the air—the Gestapo is listening and will try to locate my transmitter. Please listen closely and spread this news—the terrible things happening here—to the outside world.

Prejudice

Define *prejudice* in your own words. _____

_____

_____

_____

Find *prejudice* in a dictionary and write the definition. _____

_____

_____

_____

How are the two definitions different? _____

_____

_____

_____

How are the two definitions the same? _____

_____

_____

_____

What are four things and/or groups of people you feel have been on the receiving end of prejudice?

   1. _____   3. _____

   2. _____   4. _____

Select one of those things or groups above and explain why you think people hold that prejudice. _____

_____

_____

Do you think any prejudice is valid?_____Why or why not? _____

_____

What could you do to overcome the prejudices listed above?_____

_____

How does being prejudiced apply to the Holocaust? _____

_____

_____

_____

Literature-Related Activities

1. Read *Against All Odds: Holocaust Survivors and the Successful Lives They Made in America* by William B. Helmreich (Simon and Schuster, 1993).

   Use information from this book and from other sources of information you have to compile a list of people who survived the Holocaust and their accomplishments. A good example would be Elie Wiesel who won the Noble Peace Prize in 1986.

2. Read *Number the Stars* by Lois Lowry (Houghton Mifflin Co., 1989).

   In this story, a Christian family in Denmark risks their own lives to save the lives of a Jewish family. Discuss with the students that throughout history, there have been individuals or groups of people who have risked their lives in an effort to save others (e.g., the Underground Railroad to help free slaves in the United States). As a group, select one such effort, research it, and then create a full-page newspaper advertisement to let the world know about it. Finally, compare this effort with the efforts made to save the Jews during World War II.

   In addition to *Number the Stars*, the following books related to the Jewish resistance might be interesting and helpful:

   > *Rescue: The Story of How Gentiles Saved Jews in the Holocaust* by Milton Meltzer (HarperCollins, 1991)

   > *Raoul Wallenberg* by Michael Nicholson and David Winner (Morehouse, 1990)

3. Read *The Island on Bird Street* by Uri Orlev (Houghton Mifflin Co., 1984).

   Discuss the many struggles Alex had simply to survive. Many people throughout the world today are struggling to survive (e.g., the Bosnians in Sarajevo, the Haitians and Cubans, Chechen people in Russia).

   Ask the students to collect newspaper and magazine articles that describe the struggles that many people are facing. Make a display or collection of these articles. As a group, determine if there is something that can be done to help with others' struggles and then create and implement a plan to do something.

4. Read some of the poems and share the drawings in *I Never Saw Another Butterfly . . .* by Hana Volavkova (Schochen Books, 1978).

   After students have had the opportunity to peruse *I Never Saw Another Butterfly . . .* , ask them to create a poem with an illustration that will pay tribute to the children of Terezin and will demonstrate that they will always be remembered.

5. Read *Night* by Elie Wiesel (Bantam Books, 1986).

   Discuss the fact that many neighbors and friends stood by and watched as their Jewish friends and neighbors were persecuted. As a group, write a letter to all those people who did nothing to help.

6. Read *Alicia: My Story* by Alicia Appleman-Jurman (Bantam Books, 1988).

   Discuss with the students the fact that Alicia's non-Jewish friends and neighbors did little to help her. Create a dialog of what you think Alicia would like to say to them or what questions she might want to ask them if she talked with them today.

Literature-Related Activities *(cont.)*

7. Read *The Devil's Arithmetic* by Jan Yolen (Viking, 1988).

   Discuss the concept of the numbers that were tattooed on the arms of the prisoners in the Auschwitz concentration camp. For example, what was the purpose of the tattoo? How did the prisoners feel about being tattooed? How did the prisoners use the tattooed numbers to their benefit? How would the students feel about being tattooed for such a purpose?

8. Introduce *The Children We Remember* by Chana Byers Abells (Greenwillow, 1983).

   There are many children's and young adults' pictures included in this book. Ask the students to select one photograph of a child or young adult and respond to the following:

   a. What does the picture tell you about the person?

   b. What do you think was happening in this person(s) life prior to the picture?

   c. What do you think happened in this person(s) life after the picture?

   d. Why do you think this picture was selected to be included in this book?

   After the students have had sufficient time to respond to these questions, allow time for them to work in small groups to share the pictures they selected and their responses to the questions.

9. Read *Tell Them We Remember: The Story of the Holocaust* by Susan D. Backrach (Little, Brown, and Co., 1994).

   Read the "Afterword" on page 86. The last paragraph states that the most pressing question on one of the tiles in the Holocaust Memorial Museum wall in Washington, D.C., is "Why?" Discuss the "Why?" with your students—why and how could something as atrocious as the Holocaust happen?

10. Read *Journey to America* by Sonia Levitin (Atheneum, 1993).

    Ask the students to pretend that suddenly they are not safe living in the United States because of their ethnic background. Where would they go? What would they take with them? How soon would they leave? How would they feel? How much money would they need? Ask them to consider these questions and others and to create a short story about what their lives would be like.

11. Read *Hiding to Survive: Fourteen Jewish Children and the Gentiles Who Rescued Them from the Holocaust* by Maxine Rosenberg (Clarion, 1994).

    Ask the students to select one of the 14 first-person stories that tells how that person's childhood life was turned upside down during the Nazi regime. Once the story is selected, tell the students to summarize that person's life in a creative way through an illustration, a poem, a letter written to the person, a newspaper article, etc. Allow time for each student to share information about the person selected.

12. Read *We Remember the Holocaust* by David A. Adler (Henry Holt & Co., 1989).

    After reading *We Remember the Holocaust*, ask the students to brainstorm five ways in which people can work together to prevent a future Holocaust from occurring.

The Purpose of Passports

Directions: Throughout history there have been groups of people seeking to flee different countries because of persecution, war, revolution, and other internal upheavals. Such people are generally referred to as *refugees*—those seeking refuge or safety. As you read about the Holocaust, you may find yourself wondering why the Jews did not simply flee Germany to escape the Nazis. We have to understand, however, that Germany had invaded and occupied many of the nearby countries in Europe during World War II. Often there was no place for the Jews to go.

Moreover, in order to leave a country in which you have citizenship, you need to have official documents, such as a passport. If you are trying to escape from a hostile government, it is not always easy to get such documents. In fact, it may prove to be impossible. Then, even if you manage to secure the required documents to enter another country legally, the other country must be willing to accept you.

An illustration of the terrible situation in which Jews often found themselves is the voyage of the *S.S. St. Louis*, a German steamship. In 1939, this ship with 936 passengers aboard, almost all of whom were Jewish, sailed from Germany to Cuba to escape the Nazis. When their ship arrived in Havana, these passengers were not allowed to enter the country. Even though they held the proper visas (official permission documents), the Cuban government refused them entry.

The *S.S. St. Louis* then left Cuba, and the ship's captain requested permission from the American government to allow the passengers to enter the United States. Once again permission was denied, and the ship returned to Europe, where passengers were accepted by England, France, Holland, and Belgium. The passengers who emigrated to England were safe, but most of those accepted by the other three countries were later killed when those countries were invaded and subjugated by Nazis.

A passport allows United States citizens to travel outside the United States. It also contains a request that foreign governments protect and aid the bearer of the U.S. passport. Certain countries do not require citizens of a few other countries to have passports. United States citizens, for example, are not required to have passports to enter Canada, Mexico, or Bermuda.

All passports in the United States are issued through the State Department in Washington, D.C. The State Department maintains offices in the major cities of the country, such as Los Angeles, New York, Chicago, Philadelphia, San Francisco, Houston, Miami, etc., and applications for passports can be submitted and processed at those points also. A number of overseas diplomatic and consular offices can also legally issue passports.

Passports for citizens of Canada can be obtained at the Department of External Affairs in Ottawa.

The Purpose of Passports *(cont.)*

Directions: Fill in the blanks below as if this were your passport. Attach a small photograph of yourself in the space provided. Cut out your passport and make a cover and end sheets so that it looks like a small booklet. See if you can design an official-looking stamp for the front cover of your document.

United States of America

Passport Number

(photograph)

Surname _____
(last name)

Given names _____
(first and middle names)

Nationality_____

Date of birth _____

Sex_____

Place of birth_____

Date of issue _____

Date of expiration _____

Authority_____
(where the passport was issued)

Signature of bearer _____

Bearer's address in the United States

_____

_____

_____

Bearer's foreign address

_____

_____

_____

In case of accident or death, notify the nearest American embassy and the person listed below.

Name_____

Address _____

_____

_____

Telephone _____

Star of David

Directions: The Holocaust happened as a result of Nazi anti-Semitism (bias against Jews) and prejudice directed against people with other cultural and religious differences. During this period, all Jews were required to wear the Star of David (a star with six points that symbolizes the Jewish religion). Within the center and/or around the perimeter of the Star of David below, write six ways in which racial, religious, or ethnic prejudice can be avoided in the future. This may be done in a word, a phrase, or a short sentence.

Avenue of the Righteous

Directions: In Israel, there is a special avenue that is lined with carob trees, leading to the Holocaust Museum. This avenue is called the "Avenue of the Righteous," and each of the more than 16,000 trees planted along the avenue and the hillside behind it was planted to honor the non-Jews who risked their lives to save the Jewish people. This was a way for the Jewish people to pay a tribute to people who went out of their way to help others. On the trees below, list people to whom you would like to pay tribute. A sentence or phrase noting the reason for your selection may be added in the space remaining, according to your teacher's direction.

Note: *These can be people who have made contributions to the world as a whole or locally or simply people who have made a difference in your life.*

Avenue of the Righteous

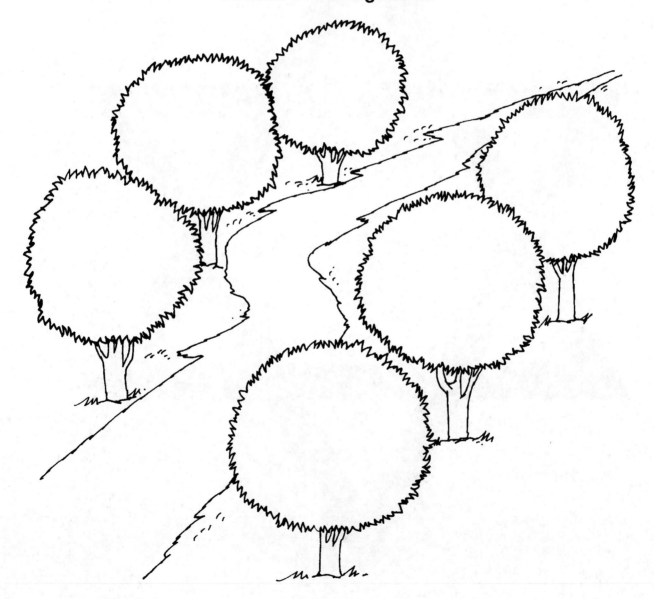

Take a Risk

Directions: Very few people helped the Jews during the Holocaust period. The United States and other countries had quotas for the number of Jewish people they would allow to immigrate. Within the European countries, many individuals were not willing to take the risk of hiding and protecting the Jewish people from the Nazis because it might put their own lives in danger. If you were put in a position to help save an innocent person's life but you knew that your own life would then be endangered, would you try to help?

- Describe what such a situation might be.

- List reasons why you would not try to help.

- List reasons why you would help.

Situation

Reasons Not to Help

Reasons to Help

Tough Times

Directions: Contributing to Hitler's rise were many economic, political, and social conditions, such as large numbers of people being unemployed, resentment for conditions following Germany's loss of World War I, and widespread religious prejudice. In the space provided below, identify as many of these conditions as possible.

Economic Conditions

_____   _____

_____   _____

_____   _____

Political Conditions

_____   _____

_____   _____

Social Conditions

_____   _____

_____   _____

Identify any of these conditions that exist in the U.S. today by placing a check beside them. Then list additional economic, political, and social conditions that exist in the U.S. today.

Economic Conditions

_____   _____

_____   _____

Political Conditions

_____   _____

_____   _____

Social Conditions

_____   _____

_____   _____

Place each of the conditions on a scale from 1 (low) to 10 (high) in level of importance. You can number the conditions and place the number before the appropriate item.

The Takeover

Directions: Use the maps on pages 63–65 to illustrate the conquest of the Germans from 1933–1944. After researching the facts, neatly label the countries shown and color red the countries that were under German control in 1933.

The Takeover *(cont.)*

Directions: After researching the facts, neatly label the countries shown and color red the countries that were under German control in 1940.

The Takeover *(cont.)*

Directions: After researching the facts, neatly label the countries shown and color red the countries that were under German control in 1944.

Nuremberg Law

Directions: The following Nuremberg Law was written and enforced, beginning in 1935. Read the Nuremberg Law and then answer the questions that follow.

Nuremberg Law for the Protection of German Blood and German Honor.

September 15, 1935

Moved by the understanding that purity of the German Blood is the essential condition for the continued existence of the German people, and inspired by the inflexible determination to ensure the existence of the German Nation for all time, the Reichstag has unanimously adopted the following Law, which is promulgated herewith:

I

1) Marriage between Jews and subjects of the state of German or related blood are forbidden. Marriages nevertheless concluded are invalid, even if concluded abroad to circumvent this law.
2) Annulment proceedings can be initiated only by the State Prosecutor.

II

Extramarital intercourse between Jews and subjects of the state of German or related blood is forbidden.

III

Jews may not employ in their households female subjects of the state of German or related blood who are under 45 years old.

IV

1) Jews are forbidden to fly the Reich or National flag or to display the Reich colors.

2) They are, on the other hand, permitted to display the Jewish colors. The exercise of this right is protected by the State.

V

1) Any person who violates the prohibition under I will be punished by a prison sentence with hard labor.
2) A male who violates the prohibition under II will be punished with a prison sentence with or without hard labor.
3) Any person violating the provisions under III or IV will be punished with a prison sentence of up to one year and a fine, or with one or the other of these penalties.
The Reich Minister of the Interior, in coordination with the Deputy of the Führer and the Reich Minister of Justice, will issue the Legal and Administrative regulations required to implement and complete the Law.
The Law takes effect on the day following promulgations except for III, which goes into force on January 1, 1936.
Nuremberg, September 15, 1935 at the Reich Party Congress of Freedom.

The Führer and Reich Chancellor
Adolf Hitler

The Reich Minister of the Interior
Frick

The Reich Minister of Justice
Dr. Gurtner

The Deputy of the Führer
R. Hess

Source: Arad, Y. et.al., Eds. *Documents on the Holocaust: Yad Vashem:* KTAV Publishing House, 1981.

Nuremberg Law *(cont.)*

1. Summarize what you think the Nuremberg Law meant for the Jewish people.

_____

_____

_____

_____

_____

_____

2. What do you find most disturbing about the Nuremberg Law?

_____

_____

_____

_____

_____

3. How would your life and the lives of your friends, family, and neighbors be different if suddenly a law such as the Nuremberg Law were imposed on your culture?

_____

_____

_____

_____

_____

4. Why do you think the Germans wrote such a law?

_____

_____

_____

_____

_____

Supplementary Activities

1. ***Schindler's List:*** View the movie *Schindler's List* with the students. (***Be certain that you have written school district approval for this activity, as well as permission slips signed by parents of each student who participates***.) Following the viewing hold a discussion in which you use the following questions:

   How do you feel about the movie?
   What is the significance of this movie?
   Who would benefit most from seeing this movie? Explain.
   Who do you think is the greatest hero of the movie? Explain.
   Why do you think the movie was done in black and white?
   What scenes were the most distressing to you? Explain.
   What did you learn about the Holocaust from this movie that you didn't already know?
   What important message should a person seeing this movie come away with?

2. **Holocaust Collage:** Using words, pictures, your own illustrations, small objects, and so forth, create a class collage that depicts the Holocaust and its atrocities.

3. **Last Witnesses:** The children who survived the Holocaust are the last witnesses of that period. If possible, invite a survivor of the Holocaust to visit your classroom. If you do not know anyone, contact the nearest Holocaust resource center. Prior to the person coming, ask the students to each think of at least one question to ask and then generate one set of meaningful and relevant questions to ask your guest.

4. **Antagonists:** As a group, discuss some current groups of people who are violently antagonistic to the governments of their countries—for example, some militia groups, skinheads, neo-Nazis, the Ku Klux Klan. Select one of these groups and write a fictional short story about what could happen if that group continues to gain strength and support.

5. **Stamp Out Prejudice:** As a group, create a campaign to stamp out bigotry, prejudice, and hate. Allow the students to create flyers, posters, newspaper and TV advertisements, etc.

6. **Persecution:** Discuss the fact that the persecution of Jewish people began many years ago—for example, the pharaohs of Egypt used Jewish slaves to build their pyramids. Ask the students to research the history of Jewish persecution and to be prepared to share their feelings.

7. **Jewish Holidays:** Obtain a calendar that indicates the various Jewish holidays—Passover, Yom Kippur, Rosh Hashanah. Ask someone who is Jewish to visit the class to explain the significance or tradition of the major holidays and how they are celebrated.

8. **Discrimination:** Ask the students to find current newspapers and magazines that depict instances of prejudice and discrimination toward a person or groups of people. If possible, invite a representative from one of the following organizations and ask him or her to discuss how the organization represented works to help eliminate prejudice and discrimination. Also, discuss how the students may become involved and assist the organization.
   National Association for the Advancement of Colored People (NAACP)
   National Conference of Christians and Jews (NCCJ)
   American Civil Liberties Union (ACLU)

9. **Holocaust Quotations:** Throughout books related to the Holocaust, there are quotes from Holocaust survivors and others. For example: "Whoever hates, hates his brother, and whenever one hates his brother, one always hates himself."
   — Elie Wiesel

   "How wonderful it is that nobody needs to wait a single moment before starting to improve the world."
   — Anne Frank

   "The first to perish were the children...From these...our new dawn might have risen."
   — Yitzhak Katzenelson

   Ask the students to select a quotation and to write a short essay on what the statement means to them. Compile the essays into a class book entitled "Quotations from the Holocaust."

10. **Holocaust Feelings:** Ask the students to reflect on the calculated killings of more than six million Jews by the Nazis during World War II and the implications for modern life. Then ask students to select a medium (essay, drawing, painting, poem, collage) to use in which they can best express their feelings about this period. Create a display or bulletin board of the projects.

Holocaust Poster

Directions: Select one of the books you have read about the Holocaust and create a poster that promotes the book. Be creative so that the poster will capture students' attention and make them want to read the book. Be sure to include the title of the book and author.

Holocaust Tile

Directions: Students from across the United States created handpainted tiles that expressed their feelings about the Holocaust. More than 3,000 of these tiles are mounted on the Wall of Remembrance in the U.S. Holocaust Memorial Museum in Washington, D.C. In the space provided below, create a tile that represents your feelings about the Holocaust.

Measure My Head

Directions: The Nazis believed the Aryan race was superior and that true Aryans had specific head measurements. Therefore, teachers were instructed to measure the heads of their students. Those with smaller heads were considered inferior (see page 12 in *Daniel's Story*).

Anthropologists, biologists, and other scientists throughout the world agree that there are some obvious physical differences among races—color, body type, hair type, eye shape, etc. However, these scientists are virtually unanimous in declaring that no single race is superior to any other. All races have members who excel at one aspect or another of human accomplishment, and all have members who do not excel.

Over the centuries, some cultures have established records of great accomplishment in certain areas—artistic, intellectual, scientific, or governmental, for example. Others have created for themselves amazing adaptations to their environments, learning to live successfully and harmoniously close to nature with little or no technological advancement. Men and women from so-called "advanced" societies, for example, would be hard put to survive for even a few days without help in the harsh environments of the equatorial rain forest, the sands of the Kalahari, or the arctic zones. Great human accomplishment is evident in all races and cultures—and that accomplishment shows itself in different ways, in different places, and at different times or ages.

From time to time in the past, some individuals (and groups) have attempted to demonstrate that one racial group or another is morally, physically, and/or intellectually "better" or "superior" to others. No such attempts, however, have survived scientific examination or careful thought. There exists no proof that any one race is "better" or "inferior" to another. And although there are differences among us, there are far more similarities binding us together as one human family.

Consider the actions of the teacher in *Daniel's Story*. On the back of this page, prepare an article for your school paper that discusses his behavior logically. You might want to think about the following questions before you start writing. When you are finished, write a final copy to turn into your teacher.

1. Suppose person A has longer arms than person B. Can we say person A is "better" than person B? Can we say that person A can probably reach farther than person B at this time?

2. Suppose person A can lift more weight than person B. Can we say that person A is "better" than person B? Can we say that person A is probably stronger than person B at this time?

3. Suppose person A solves math problems faster and more accurately than person B. Can we say that person A is "better" than person B? Can we say that person A is probably more skilled in math than person B right now?

4. Now, suppose person A has a larger head than person B. Can we say that person A is "better" than person B? Can we say that person A is "smarter" than person B? Can we say person A will probably need a larger hat size than person B?

Facts and Figures

Directions: Solve the following problems by using facts and figures provided from Holocaust books, atlases, encyclopedias, and other sources.

1. If Adolf Hitler became Chancellor of Germany in 1933 and is believed to have committed suicide in 1945, how many years was he in power? _____

2. How many years was the U.S. involved in World War II? _____

3. Anne Frank was born in Frankfurt am Main, Germany, in 1929. She then moved to Amsterdam, the Netherlands, in 1934. How long did she live in Germany? _____

4. Using a mileage legend on a map, estimate the number of miles Anne Frank would have traveled when she moved from Frankfurt am Main, Germany, to Amsterdam in the Netherlands.

    _____

5. Anne Frank was moved by the Germans from Amsterdam to Westerbork, from Westerbork to Auschwitz-Birkenau, and then to Bergen-Belsen where she died. Estimate the number of miles Anne would have traveled while she was a prisoner of the Germans. _____

6. How many European countries had the Nazis occupied by 1940? _____

7. How many years did Anne Frank write in her diary? _____

8. Millions of Jewish people were killed in as many as 22 different European countries during World War II. After researching for the facts, create a graph showing the number of Jewish people killed in each of the following countries: Austria, Greece, Germany, Poland, Latvia, Netherlands, France, Lithuania, Hungary, Czechoslovakia, Romania, the Soviet Union, Yugoslavia. A sample graph format that may be used appears below.

Countries	Jewish Holocaust Deaths
Austria	
Greece	
Germany	
Poland	
Latvia	
Netherlands	
France	
Lithuania	
Hungary	
Czechoslovakia	
Romania	
Soviet Union	
Yugoslavia	

Each mark on the graph represents 100,000 human beings.

Facts and Figures *(cont.)*

9. In which European country were the most Jews killed?_____ How many?_____

   In which European country were the least Jews killed?_____ How many?_____
   How many total Jews were killed by the end of the war in all European countries?_____

10. List the other groups of people besides the Jews who were killed during the Holocaust period and estimate the number killed in each of the groups.

    Groups killed _____ _____ _____ _____ _____

    Number killed _____ _____ _____ _____ _____

11. More than 17 million of those who served in the Allied and Axis armed forces lost their lives in the war. The chart below lists the number of military deaths and missing in action for some of the countries involved. Use the information to answer the questions that follow.

Allies Countries	Deaths
Australia	29,400
Belgium	8,000
Canada	39,000
China	1,400,000
France	122,000
Great Britain	305,000
Greece	1,830
Soviet Union	11,000,000
United States	405,400
Total	

Axis Countries	Deaths
Bulgaria	32,000
Finland	89,000
Germany	3,250,000
Hungary	136,000
Italy	226,900
Japan	1,740,000
Romania	300,000
Total	

A. Which group had the greater number of deaths—Allies or Axis? _____

B. What is the difference between the number of deaths for Allies and Axis?_____

C. Which Allied country suffered the most casualties? _____

D. Which Axis country suffered the most casualties? _____

E. How many more deaths did Great Britain suffer than Italy? _____

F. How many more deaths did the Soviet Union suffer than Germany?_____

G. How many fewer deaths did France suffer than Romania?_____

H. How many fewer deaths did Hungary suffer than the United States? _____

I. List the Allied countries with fewer than 400,000 deaths. _____

J. List the Axis countries with fewer than 150,000 deaths. _____

Concluding the Holocaust

1. Ask the students to reflect on what they have learned about the Holocaust since they first started the unit. Ask them to think about what they still do not understand or know. Have them fold a sheet of paper in half lengthwise. On the outside ask them to title it "Knowledge of the Holocaust." On the left inside page, write the heading "What I Know About the Holocaust." On the facing inside page, have them write "What I Would Like to Know About the Holocaust." Finally, tell them to complete the two sections, listing neatly all the information they can. Lastly, have them design a border or front page graphic for their folders.

2. Schedule a "Remember the Holocaust Day" that might coincide with the national "Holocaust Remembrance Week" that is usually held in April. Contact the U.S. Holocaust Memorial Museum, 100 Raoul Wallenberg Place, S.W., Washington, DC 20024-2150, to get information on what activities are designed for this special week. Then create your own day that might include the following displays and activities:

- Share the poems, essays, posters, facts, figures, and other products that were created during the study of the Holocaust.

- Collect and display these products in folders titled "We Remember." Include ads and newspaper or magazine layouts telling why a National Holocaust Memorial Museum is important to all the world—not just those places where the tragedy occurred.

- Share as many as possible of the students' books related to the Holocaust.

- Put up maps of Europe, indicating territory occupied by Germany prior to Hitler (1932) and again at the end of his era (1945) to indicate the amount of control the Nazis had.

- Hold a design competition for a permanent memorial statue or monument commemorating this somber historical tragedy. Display the entries for visitors to share and perhaps help judge.

- Invite parents, other students, school administrators, and community members to this special day.

3. Assist the students in completing "Holocaust Who's Who" (page 75), "Holocaust Words" (page 76), and "Holocaust Courage" (page 77). Allow time to share.

Holocaust Who's Who

Directions: During and after the Holocaust, there were a number of people who became well known because of their actions—both good and bad. Read each of the descriptions below and see how many of these people you can identify. Use the names in the box at the bottom of the page to assist you.

_____ 1. The head of the Gestapo section for Jewish affairs

_____ 2. The Chancellor of Germany, appointed in 1933

_____ 3. The Nazi leader who wrote the memo asking an SS officer to prepare a plan for the "Final Solution of the Jewish Problem"—mass extermination

_____ 4. General of U.S. armed forces during World War II

_____ 5. A man who helped to save tens of thousands of Jews in Hungary in 1944 by creating special passports with the Swedish seal, granting immunity to those who held them

_____ 6. A Holocaust victim who survived and became the recipient of the 1986 Nobel Peace Prize

_____ 7. A young girl who died in the Holocaust but whose memories survive through the diary she kept

_____ 8. The Chief of the SS, the private army of the Nazi Party

_____ 9. The man who invented an early version of the modern computer

_____ 10. A man who saved the lives of many Jewish men, women, and children

---

• Adolf Hitler	• Raoul Wallenberg
• Adolf Eichmann	• Anne Frank
• Hermann Goering	• Dwight David Eisenhower
• Elie Wiesel	• Oskar Schindler
• Heinrich Himmler	• Herman Hollerith

Holocaust Words

Draw a six-sided star to represent the Star of David on the chalkboard or overhead projector. Inside the star, write the following vocabulary words and others that the students might suggest:

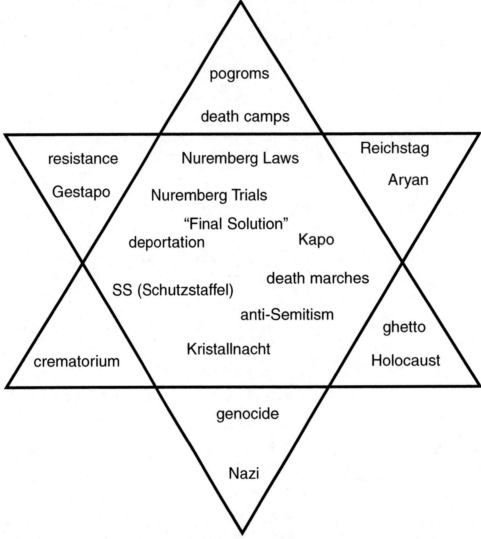

- Assign a pair of students to each word. After they have been given a few minutes to review their words, ask them to explain what the word means and how it relates to the Holocaust.

- After this exercise is completed, ask the students to think of different categories in which to classify the words (e.g., *Death Words*, *Injustice Words*). Write these categories on the chalkboard. Then assign the pairs of students to work together classifying the words.

- Next, as a whole group, work together to decide on the classification of these words as the teacher writes them under the designated categories. **Note:** *Students may come up with new categories when they begin the classification activity.*

- Ask one student to write all the vocabulary words on small slips of paper that can be folded and placed in a box.

- Then, as a follow-up to the definition and classification activity, put the words in a box, draw three words from the box and ask the students to write a sentence that contains the three words selected. Ask for volunteers to share sentences. Continue until all words have been used.

Holocaust Courage

Throughout history there have been many people who exhibited great courage. In the study of the Holocaust, both non-Jews and Jews showed great courage. Think about what courage means to you and complete the following:

1. To me, *courage* is _____.

2. The dictionary definition of *courage* is _____.

3. The person I believe exhibited the greatest courage during the Holocaust was _____.

4. What characteristics made this person courageous? _____

   _____

   _____

   _____

   _____

5. What person do you know (or currently know of) whom you consider courageous?

   _____

6. What characteristics make this person courageous?

   _____

   _____

   _____

   _____

7. Is it possible to have courage in one aspect of your life and not in others? _____

   Explain: _____

   _____

   _____

   _____

8. In the space provided, create a badge that you feel would both symbolize and honor the quality of courage—a badge fitting to be awarded to a person who demonstrated courage through some action in his or her life.

Bibliography

Abells, Chana Byers. *The Children We Remember*. Greenwillow, 1983.

Ackerman, Karen. *The Night Crossing*. Alfred Knopf, 1994.

Adler, David A. *We Remember the Holocaust*. Henry Holt & Co., 1989.

Appleman-Jurman, Alicia. *Alicia: My Story*. Bantam, 1988.

Backrach, Susan D. *Tell Them We Remember*. Little, Brown & Co., 1994.

Bernbaum, Israel. *My Brother's Keeper: The Holocaust Through the Eyes of an Artist*. Putnam, 1985.

Bernheim, Mark. *Father of the Orphans: The Story of Janusz Korczak*. Dutton, 1989.

Black, Wallace and Jean Blashfield. *Victory in Europe*. Crestwood House, 1993.

Bunting, Eve. *Terrible Things: An Allegory of the Holocaust*. Jewish Publication Society, 1989.

Chaikin, Miriam. *A Nightmare in History: The Holocaust, 1933–1945*. Clarion, 1987.

Drucker, Olga Levy. *Kindertransport*. Henry Holt & Co., 1992.

Finkelstein, Norman H. *Remember Not to Forget*. Franklin Watts, 1985.

Friedrich, Otto. *The Kingdom of Auschwitz*. HarperCollins, 1994.

Genrts, Barbara. *Don't Say a Word*. Macmillan, 1986.

Greensfield, Howard. *The Hidden Children*. Ticknor and Fields, 1993.

Isaacman, Clara and Joan Grossman. *Clara's Story*. Jewish Publication Society, 1984.

Laird, Christa. *Shadow of the Wall*. Greenwillow, 1990.

Landau, Elaine. *The Warsaw Ghetto Uprising*. New Discovery Books, 1992.

Leitner, Isabella and Irving. *The Big Lie: A True Story*. Scholastic, 1992.

Levitin, Sonia. *Journey to America*. Atheneum, 1993.

Lowry, Lois. *Number the Stars*. Houghton Mifflin, 1989.

Matas, Carol. *Lisa's War*. Charles Scribner's Sons, 1989.

Neimark, Anne. *One Man's Valor: Leo Baeck and the Holocaust*. Dutton, 1986.

Nicholson, Michael and David Winner. *Raoul Wallenberg*. Ridgefield, Morehouse, 1990.

Orlev, Uri. *The Island on Bird Street*. Houghton Mifflin, 1984.

Orlev, Uri. *The Man from the Other Side*. Houghton Mifflin, 1991.

Reiss, Johanna. *The Upstairs Room*. HarperCollins, 1990.

Richter, Hans. *Friedrich*. Puffin, 1987.

Rogasky, Barbara. *Smoke and Ashes: The Story of the Holocaust*. Holiday House, 1989.

Rosenberg, Maxine. *Hiding to Survive: Fourteen Stories of Jewish Children Rescued by Gentiles from the Holocaust*. Clarion, 1994.

Rossel, Seymour. *The Holocaust*. Franklin Watts, 1989.

Roth-Hano, Renee. *Touch Wood: A Girlhood in Occupied France*. Puffin Books, 1989.

Sender, Ruth. *The Cage*. Macmillan, 1986.

Sender, Ruth. *The Holocaust Lady*. Macmillan, 1992.

Volavkova, Hana, ed. *I Never Saw Another Butterfly: Children's Drawings and Poems from Terezin Concentration Camp, 1942–1944*. Schocken, 1993.

Vos, Ida. *Anna Is Still Here*. Houghton Mifflin, 1993.

Vos, Ida. *Hide and Seek*. Houghton Mifflin, 1993.

Wiesel, Elie. *Night*. Bantam, 1982.

Yolen, Jan. *The Devil's Arithmetic*. Viking, 1988.

Resource Materials

Holocaust videos, study and discussion guides, curricula, exhibits, and books are available from the following publishers and companies: (Write and request a catalog of their Holocaust materials.)

Anne Frank Institute of Philadelphia
(215-625-0411)
431 Chestnut Street
Lafayette Bldg, Suite 211
Philadelphia, PA 19106

Holocaust Education and Memorial
Center of Toronto
(416-635-2883)
4600 Bathurst Street
Willowdale, Ontario, M2R-3V2
Canada

Anti-Defamation League of B'nai B'rith
(212-490-2525)
823 United Nations Plaza
New York, NY 10017

Holocaust Memorial Resource and Educational Center of Central Florida
(305-628-0555)
851 North Maitland Avenue
Maitland, FL 32751

Association of Holocaust Organizations
Dallas Memorial Center for the Holocaust
(214-750-4654)
7900 Horthhaven Road
Dallas, TX 75230

Holocaust Resource Center Archives
Queensborough Community College
Bayside, NY 11364

CRM (619-495-2327)
22215 Faraday, Suite F
Carlsbad, CA 92008

Jewish Labor Committee
(212-477-0707)
25 East 21st Street
New York, NY 10010

Ergo Media, Inc.
(800-695-3746)
P.O. Box 2037
Teaneck, NJ 07666

Leo Baeck Institute
(212-744-6400)
129 East 73rd Street
New York, NY 10021

Gratz College Holocaust
Oral History Archive
(215-329-3363)
10th and Tabor Road
Philadelphia, PA 19141

Living Voices
(206-328-0798)
915 East Pine, Suite 405
Seattle, WA 98122

Jewish Heritage Project, Inc.
(212-925-9067)
150 Franklin Street, #1 W
New York, NY 10003

Martyrs Memorial and Museum of the Holocaust
(213-852-1234)
6505 Wilshire Blvd.
Los Angeles, CA 90048

The National Catholic Center for Holocaust Education
Holocaust Education-Seton Hill College
(412-834-2200, Ext. 344)
Seton Hill Drive
Greensburg, PA 15601

Video Archive for Holocaust
Testimonies at Yale
(203-436-2157)
Sterling Memorial Library,
Rm. 331C
Yale University
New Haven, CT 06520

New York Holocaust Memorial Commission
(212-867-5020)
342 Madison Avenue, Suite 717
New York, NY 10017

Warsaw Ghetto Resistance Organization
(212-564-1065)
122 West 30th Street
New York, NY 10001

New York Films Video
(212-247-6110)
16 West 61st Street
New York, NY 10023

Zenger Video
(800-421-4246)
10200 Jefferson Blvd., Rm. 902
P.O. Box 802
Culver City, CA 90232

PBS Video
(800-344-3337)
1320 Braddock Place
Alexandria, VA 22314

Phoenix-BFA Films and Video
(314-569-0211)
2349 Chaffee Drive
St. Louis, MO 63146

Simon Wiesenthal Center
(310-553-9036)
Yeshiva University of Los Angeles
9760 West Pico Blvd.
Los Angeles, CA 90035

U.S. Holocaust Memorial Museum
(202-488-0400)
100 Raoul Wallenberg Pl. SW
Washington, DC 20004-2150

National Yiddish Book Center
(Aaron Lansky, Founder)
Amherst, Massachusetts

Holocaust
(800-831-9183)
Blackbirch Press
260 Amity Road
Woodbridge, CT 06525

Answer Key

Page 12, Holocaust Crossword Puzzle

Across

1. Auschwitz
4. Nuremberg Laws
8. Resistance
9. Axis
11. Allies
12. Synagogue
13. Labor Camps
14. Pogrom
15. Hitler

Down

2. Crematoria
3. Aryan
5. Bar Mitzvah
6. Ghetto
7. Kristallnacht
10. Gestapo

Page 32, What Is a Mensch?

e 1.
c 2.
g 3.
a 4.
d 5.
b 6.
j 7.
i 8.
h 9.
f 10.

Page 41, Crack the Code

Statement	1	2	3	4	5	6	7	8	9	10	11	12	13	14
True	P	E	M	S	A	D	K	N	X	O	R	W	E	O
False	O	Q	T	I	N	L	R	U	G	V	E	C	K	C

Write the circled letters in the blanks below to find out an important message concerning the Holocaust. For example, the first statement is false, and therefore the letter "O" is circled and the letter "O" is written above the numeral 1.

N O M O R E G E N O C I D E
5 1 3 14 7 2 9 13 8 10 12 4 6 11

Page 43, Fact or Opinion

1. F   10. F
2. O   11. O
3. O   12. O
4. F   13. F
5. F   14. F
6. O   15. O
7. F
8. F
9. O

Pages 72 and 73, Facts and Figures

1. 12 years
2. 4 years
3. 5 years
4. approximately 500 miles
5. approximately 1,500 miles
6. 6 countries
7. 2 years
8.

Austria	65,000
Greece	71,300
Germany	160,000
Poland	3,000,000
Latvia	80,000
The Netherlands	106,000
France	83,000
Lithuania	135,000
Hungary	305,000
Czechoslovakia	270,000
Romania	365,000
Soviet Union	1,000,000
Yugoslavia	67,000

9. Poland—3,000,000
   Finland—11
   All European Countries—6,000,000
10. Answers may vary
11.
   A. Allies
   B. 7,536,730
   C. Soviet Union
   D. Germany
   E. 78,100
   F. 7,750,000
   G. 178,000
   H. 269,400
   I. Australia, Belgium, Canada, France, Great Britain, Greece
   J. Bulgaria, Finland, Hungary

Page 75, Holocaust Who's Who

1. Adolf Eichmann
2. Adolf Hitler
3. Hermann Goering
4. Dwight David Eisenhower
5. Raoul Wallenberg
6. Elie Wiesel
7. Anne Frank
8. Heinrich Himmler
9. Herman Hollerith
10. Oskar Schindler